THE RELATIONSHIP BETWEEN RACE-RELATED STRESS AND THE CAREER PLANNING AND CONFIDENCE FOR AFRICAN-AMERICAN COLLEGE STUDENTS

THE RELATIONSHIP BETWEEN RACE-RELATED STRESS AND THE CAREER PLANNING AND CONFIDENCE FOR AFRICAN-AMERICAN COLLEGE STUDENTS

Dwaine Turner PhD, CRC

To order additional copies of this book, contact:
Xlibris
1-888-795-4274
www.Xlibris.com
Orders@Xlibris.com
796453

THE RELATIONSHIP BETWEEN RACE-RELATED STRESS AND THE CAREER PLANNING AND CONFIDENCE FOR AFRICAN-AMERICAN COLLEGE STUDENTS

by

Dwaine Tito Turner

A thesis submitted in partial fulfillment
of the requirements for the Doctor of Philosophy
degree in Rehabilitation and Counselor Education
in the Graduate College of
The University of Iowa

August 2015

Thesis Supervisor: Associate Professor Noel Estrada-Hernández

Graduate College
The University of Iowa
Iowa City, Iowa

CERTIFICATE OF APPROVAL

_____

PH.D. THESIS

_____

This is to certify that the Ph.D. thesis of

Dwaine Tito Turner

has been approved by the Examining Committee for
the thesis requirement for the Doctor of Philosophy degree
in Rehabilitation and Counselor Education at the August 2015 graduation.

Thesis Committee: _____
                     Noel Estrada-Hernández, Thesis Supervisor

                     _____
                     John S. Wadsworth

                     _____
                     Vilia M. Tarvydas

                     _____
                     Timothy Ansley

                     _____
                     Stewart Ehly

ACKNOWLEDGEMENTS

First and foremost all praise goes to my lord and savior Jesus Christ for blessing me with the resiliency and determination to complete the requirements for my degree, and for sending me so many kind and generous people without whom I would have been lost on this path. It may take a village to raise a child; I think it scarcely takes less to raise a dissertation. To my mother, Sandra Braswell and auntie, Dr. Carolyn Kornegay who kept me grounded when I was at my lowest point and when I was at my highest, all my love, always. To the loving memory of Dorothy L. Been, George Been and Samuel T. Braswell I wish you all were still here…your memories will always shine deep inside of me. I would like to thank the professors Dr. Estrada, Dr. Wadsworth, Dr. Tarvydas, Dr. Ansley and Dr. Ehly that have been instrumental in guiding and pushing along the way to fulfill my dream. The list of others is far too long to go through but they know who they are and the special place they hold in my heart.

ABSTRACT

The literature on multiculturalism and career counseling (Harro, 2010) has extensively documented the role and influence of environments such as schools in the perpetuation of behavioral attitudes like discrimination and racism. Indeed, researchers have suggested that early experiences of racial discrimination in school may lead African-Americans to believe that their education will not benefit them (O'Hara et. al., 2011). They may perceive that racial barriers will hold them back regardless of hard work.

It is of great importance that rehabilitation, school, and college counselors understand the effects of racism on the lives of African-American students to avoid permitting it to lead to academic underachievement and low participation in higher education. This includes the effects of stress related experiences of racism on the attainment of a vocational or career goal. This study of African American college students at a predominantly White institution explores the relationship between race-related stress and participants' occupational planning and confidence.

Many of the participants have demonstrated elements of what Lent, Brown, and Hackett (2000) identify as self-efficacy in that the majority have already selected an area of academic concentration for their bachelor's degree, many of them in careers of high demand like engineering. Thus, the career selection process is likely underway. Results of the analysis reveal that they consider it important to consider race-related stress in choosing a career, but that race-related stress does not affect their career confidence. However, their low scores and negative correlations in the Career Planning area suggest they have done little to achieve a career path beyond selecting a field of study. The study does not address whether this omission reflects interest or opportunity, as access to resources like career counseling or guidance is outside its scope. Future research should replicate this study with a larger sample size and with access to resources addressed. Nonetheless it provides a significant contribution in exploring the potential relationship between experiencing race-related stress and the selection and implementation of a career plan.

PUBLIC ABSTRACT

This research study addresses three types of race-related stress its participants may face during the career development process: individual, cultural, and institutional. All three reflect a traditional expectation that African-Americans will select career paths that require manual labor and other skills, but not a higher education degree. The study addresses the impact of all three types of racism in the three areas of developing a career planning, believing in its importance and confidence.

Existing research suggests that, as with all demographics in college, some African-Americans seek the services of a career counselor as a crucial part of career planning. However, traditional counseling tenets based on procedures implemented originally to serve Caucasian males may not address others' needs; in the case of African-American students, this may reflect deficiencies in understanding of the nature of racism. Findings from this study have the possibility of providing counselors the tools they need to remedy this deficiency by identifying the values and beliefs African-American young adults hold dear to ensure they will be empowered to overcome barriers that might impede their progression to enroll and complete college and ultimately in the world of work.

CONTENTS

LIST OF TABLES

LIST OF FIGURES

CHAPTER I

INTRODUCTION

Race-related stress occurs in many forms, all of which produce barriers to success for African-Americans in their pursuit of education and social mobility. As Harrell (2000, p.44) sums up a broad area of feelings, race-related stress includes "race-related transactions between individuals or groups and their environment that emerge from the dynamics of racism, and that are perceived to tax or exceed existing individual and collective resources or threaten well-being". In general, this variety of stressors falls into three categories: individual, institutional, and cultural. In relation to education, individual stressors include social economic status, level of parental education, role model/mentoring, and occupational exposure. African-Americans face institutional stressors when their schools fail to support them in the pursuit of high-status careers. Cultural stressors enter the field when an individual's cultural perspective on education and certain professions makes it difficult for them to pursue particular goals.

The literature on multiculturalism and career counseling (Harro, 2010) has extensively documented the role and influence of environments such as school in the perpetuation of behavioral attitudes like discrimination and racism. Researchers have suggested that early racial discrimination experiences in school may lead African-Americans to believe that they cannot obtain a professional career or steady employment because of racial barriers, and that therefore education will not benefit them (O'Hara et. al., 2011). They argue that these experiences make African-American students likely to take the path of academic underachievement and low participation in higher education.

It is, therefore, of great importance that rehabilitation, school, and college counselors understand the effects of racism on the lives of African-Americans. These include the effects of stress related to the potential experiences of racism on the attainment of vocational or career goals. This study explores the relationship between race-related stress and the career planning and confidence of African-American college students in a predominantly White institution, as a means to provide such information.

Chapter I provides an overview of perceived race-related stress, particularly as it relates to career planning for African-Americans. It also provides a presentation of the theoretical framework used in this study. Chapter I concludes with the purpose statement, guiding research questions, and definitions of relevant terms associated with the present study.

Overview

Career Counseling for African Americans

Fouad and Byars-Winston define career counseling as "the process of assisting individuals in the development of a life-career with a focus on the definition of the worker role and how that role interacts with other life roles" (2005, p.224). Through the process of career development, consumers work with a career counselor to help clarify the process through which contextual barriers and skill development become internalized (Lent, Brown, & Hackett, 2000). Career barriers are those conditions or events that impede people's progress in their careers, and include internal and external conditions (Swanson & Woitke, 1997).

A career barrier is generic, ever present, and transcends choice domains and developmental considerations (Lent, Brown, & Hackett, 2000). Coincidently, some environmental conditions can become salient in creating a career goal than actual pursuit of an initial goal

The Relationship Between Race-Related Stress and the Career
Planning and Confidence for African-American College Students

3

(Lent, Brown, & Hackett, 2000). According to, Lent, Brown and Hackett (2000), the reason for this phenomenon is due to the fact that obtaining goals may expose the individual to possible financial problems or discrimination that was not anticipated during the creation of goal.

Contemporary literature attests that race-related stress plays a crucial role in African American college students' vocational choices (Tovar-Murray, Jenifer, Andrusyk, D'Angelo, & King, 2012). Researchers have also shown that racism and minority racial identity can undermine individuals' abilities to reach specific vocational goals, and that stronger racial identity for African-Americans increases the effect (Tovar-Murray et. al., 2012). Increases in race-related stress among African-American college students correlate with aspirations of lower status held occupations, but even those with stronger held aspirations encounter race-related challenges in pursuit of vocational choice (Tovar-Murray et. al., 2012). Career counselors at U.S. colleges have begun to implement sociocultural contexts into their sessions with African- American students as a means of identifying barriers these students face in goal setting and pursuit (Tovar-Murray et. al., 2012).

Research suggests African-American adolescents and teens choose career paths that align with their racial identity and career readiness, which suggests counselors, should possess cultural knowledge to understand clients' value systems (Parham, & Austin, 1994). Outcome expectations influence an individual's willingness to expend energy towards the pursuit of a career goals, and racial identity influence expectations (Parham, & Austin, 1994). Fouad and Byars-Winston's (2005) study of students at a few of U.S. colleges identifies the crucial need for counselors to understand the influence of race/ethnicity on career aspirations.

While the study found no major difference in career aspirations among ethnic groups, ethnic groups showed differences in exposure to career-related opportunities and barriers, and that race/ethnicity greatly influenced perception of career barriers. Results include the fact that African American identity positively correlated with the belief that education would effectively change social-economic status. Other variables the study addressed include age, disability status, spiritual beliefs, gender, and sexual orientation, all of which correlated with exposure and perception for students (Fouad, & Byars-Winston, 2005).

The study concluded that career counselors should use culture-specific counseling interventions to help clients from diverse cultures, even though contemporary research on cultural variables have not identified their influence on successful career decision making and career counseling, because consumers seek career counseling that incorporates their views, values, and worldviews to influence their vocational choice (Fouad, & Byars-Winston, 2005). Earlier research suggests that differences with respect to these cultural aspects of students are the source of conflicts in counseling sessions, so modifications would be warranted on this basis along (Sue, 1977). Furthermore, recent research suggests individuals of lower socioeconomic status feel a need to find employment quickly, and that this negates the sense that careful career planning confers a benefit (Lent, 2013).

Older research suggests that the perception that high school and college counselors offer career advice inappropriate to African-Americans have led young people to seek career advice from institutions such as churches and community centers, where they expect advice free of discriminatory messages and with their lived experiences as the central context for advice (Parham, & Austin, 1994). Traditional career counseling theories and models (1) assume equal opportunities exist for obtaining vocational goals; (2) Career theories and models overview of concepts and constructs based on white majority behavior to ethnic and economic subgroups; (3) Several theories of career development relies on the conjecture that an occupation provides a person with basic contentment and opportunities for manifestation of self (Hendricks, 1994). Including culture-specific variables in counseling sessions allows counselors to understand culture-specific meanings of sociopolitical, historical, and political experiences in regards to work (Fouad, & Byars-Winston, 2005).

The fabric of African-Americans' daily life activities reflect religious, spiritual, and communal values that may differ from white students' (Constantine, Warren, Gainor, & Lewis-Coles, 2006). Religious beliefs, values, and practices serve as vital background on students thoughts, feelings, experiences, and behaviors related to career development (Constantine et. al., 2006).Recognizing that work is a vital part of culture and family maintenance requires differentiated approaches (Fouad, & Byars-Winston, 2005). The value and expectations of work hold different meanings across ethnicities, functioning as sociocultural, historical, and political experiences that comprise the outlook on the structure of occupational opportunities (Fouad, & Byars-Winston, 2005).

Factoring in such values can empower the individual with a better understanding of the processes of contextual barriers as an impediment to skills acquisition and provide counseling and tools for coping or adapting to environmental barriers (Lent, Brown, & Hackett, 2000). Counselors should be able to recognize correct intervention targets and advocate for an individual's negative contextual influences (Lent, Brown, & Hackett, 2000). Effective counseling empowers individuals to recognize distinct barriers and address them, and thus provides beneficial support in chosen careers (Lent, Brown, & Hackett, 2000). Individuals receive a benefit in the sense of (a) making specific choices that help them overcome barriers, (b) distinguishing proximal and distant variables of the environment, (c) pondering the association of barriers to relevant variables, (d) reassuring clients that barriers interact with outcome agenda and time frame, (e) studying positive environmental surroundings or support (Lent, Brown, & Hackett, 2000).

Career Planning and Confidence

Career planning is the process through which individuals evaluate their career opportunities, decide on their career goals and take advantage of developmental opportunities to reach their identified goals (Sonmez, & Yildirim, 2009). Individuals are accountable for defining their own developmental needs and integrating them with current career opportunities (Sonmez, & Yildirim, 2009). Jesse Buttrick Davis was first person to respond to students' need for guidance in these processes by implementing a systemic guidance program in schools in the United States, in the 1800s (Pope, 2009).

Davis' career development theories were based on the Euro-American male. Evidence suggests that for African-Americans, self-esteem may be separate from their academic achievement (O'Hare et al., 2011). For African-American students who decide to continue their education past high school, the transition to college or professional school may increase race-related stress and students face social setbacks and isolation (Walton, & Cohen, 2011).

Racism

Harrell (2000, p. 43) defines racism as "a system of dominance, power, and privilege based on racial-group designations; rooted in historical oppression of a group defined or perceived by dominant-group members as inferior, deviant, or undesirable; and occurring in circumstances where members of the dominant group create or accept their societal privilege by maintaining structures, ideology, values, and behavior that have the intent or effect of leaving non-dominant-group members relatively excluded from power, esteem, status, and/or equal access to societal resources" Harrell categorizes racism as individual, institutional, and cultural (Harrell, 2000). Individual racism can take the form of belief in the inferiority of a racial/ethnic group (Harrell, 2000). Institutional racism refers to systemic oppression and exploitation (Harrell, 2000). Cultural racism is ethnocentrism and status-quo maintenance (Harrell, 2000).

Individual, institutional, and cultural racism can also be apparent in four contexts: interpersonal, collective, cultural-symbolic, and sociopolitical. When it occurs in interpersonal contexts, the individual experiences racism through the verbal or non-verbal behavior of other individuals, either directly or vicariously (Harrell, 2000). Cultural and institutional racism creates environmental support for individual behavior in interpersonal circumstances, but interpersonal racism may also be individual (Harrell, 2000).

The collective context reflects the inequalities of a group; examples include educational achievement, unemployment rates, incidence and prevalence of disease, and criminal justice treatment. These inequalities replicate the continuous effects of individual, cultural, and institutional racism (Harrell, 2000). Racism continues to grow because of the status and function of the majority of a large group of people (Harrell, 2000). Racism in the cultural-symbolic context uses descriptions and imprints of non-dominant racial/ethnic groups through media outlets such as news and entertainment (Harrell, 2000). Art, literature, research, and scientific investigation enacts racism in a cultural-symbolic context (Harrell, 2000). Racism in a sociopolitical context plays out in race philosophy policies and government practices within societies (Harrell, 2000). Examples include racial profiling, differential treatment within criminal courts, and resource distribution within education.

According to Harro (2010), early experiences with racism have a damaging effect on individuals' social outcomes. The relevance of racism to career planning itself comes in many forms. African-American parents typically know their children have unequal access to educational, social, and vocational areas because of racism, and factor this into their parenting, which can in turn shape children's approach to career (Constantine, Wallace, & Kindaichi, 2005). As Harrell (2000) points out, individual physical characteristics like skin color, hair texture, body shape, speech patterns and facial features vary among different racial/ethnic groups and can influence the intensity and type of racism people experience; this the effects or racism on career planning can vary. Ultimately, race-related stress affects the career planning of most people of color.

Race-Related Stress

Race-related stress can take on many forms that can produce barriers to success for African Americans who strive to better themselves through education. Documented effects of racism in the form of academic discrimination extend back at least to 5th grade for African Americans (O'Hara et. al., 2011). Harrell (2000) identifies six forms: life events, vicarious experiences, daily micro-stressors, chronic-contextual stress, collective experiences of, and trans-generational transmission of group traumas (Harrell).

This section will outline each of these forms, relate them to individual, institutional, and cultural types of racism, and address findings in the literature with respect to African-American understandings of education. Racism-related life events reflect significant life events that are time-limited that can manifest into other events, which may have lasting effects (Harrell). These experiences can happen in neighborhood, work, finances, education, law enforcement/legal, healthcare, and social environments (Harrell).

Personal and environmental factors that occur on a daily or weekly basis influence these events. Vicarious racism experiences take place through personal knowledge and vicarious reflection and report (Harrell). This type of vicarious experience may increase anxiety, anger, sadness, and emotional and psychological reactions (Harrell). Through such experiences, individuals distinguish between overt and covert racism. Like racism-related life events, vicarious racism experiences impose episodic stress on individuals (Harrell).

Daily racism micro-stressors serve as reminders that race is an ongoing stimulus in the world (Harrell). Micro-stressors can take the form of receiving inferior customer service or being identified as a service industry worker (Harrell). African-Americans can experience such micro-stressors on a regular basis. Chronic-contextual stress reflects social structure, political dynamics, and institutional racism on social-role demands and environment with which one has to cope and adapt (Harrell).

This type of stress can take the form of inadequate dissemination of capital and limits the opportunities for people from ethnic minority groups. Collective experiences reflect the involvement of racism at the group level where individuals can detect cultural-symbolic and socio-political displays of racism (Harrell). The welfare of individuals with limited personal familiarities of racism can be affected by observation of the effects on the lives of others with which they have an association and identification (Harrell). Trans-generational transmission refers to the history of a racial group's effects on the relationship between the group and the wider American society (Harrell).

THE RELATIONSHIP BETWEEN RACE-RELATED STRESS AND THE CAREER
PLANNING AND CONFIDENCE FOR AFRICAN-AMERICAN COLLEGE STUDENTS

9

Throughout history, racial groups have passed down stories that have molded understanding of racism in U.S. society (Harrell). Chronic-contextual stress, collective experiences, and trans-generational transmission of race-related stress all impose chronic strain on individuals (Harrell). Race–related stress, like the racism that causes it, has individual, institutional, and cultural facets. Its individual facet includes the eroding of hopes to continue education, pursue careers, and acceptance of unwanted behavior (O'Hara et. al., 2011). For college students, institutional stress may include institutional characteristics such as the number of minority faculty in the school they attend. Cultural stress can be defined as cultural views passed on through several generations about education, peer-based, and societal stereotypes.

Several studies influence the importance of cultural values for young people, such as a study that reveals its role in the decision to attend college (Phinney, Dennis, & Osorio, 2006). O'Hara et al. (2011) noted that personal racial discrimination experiences explain the disparity between African Americans and European Americans in areas of academic achievement. A report commissioned by the Bill and Melinda Gates Foundation (2008) indicated that only 55% of all African American students graduated from high school compared to 78% of European Americans. Additionally, in 2006, only 19% of African Americans had bachelor's degrees, while only 1% had advanced degrees (Caldwell & Obasi, 2010).

Caldwell & Obasi (2010) offered the explanation that African-Americans feel they do not have an equal opportunity in the United States and therefore devalue academic achievement. However, African-Americans report valuing education with greater strength than their European American counterparts (O'Hara et. al., 2011). This suggests barriers like racism or race-related stress might play a stronger role than a failure to value academic achievement itself (Tovar-Murray et al., 2011).

Theoretical Framework

This study of the perceived race-related stress that faces a sample of African-American college students enrolled at a predominately white university and the impact of this stress on their career planning will use Bandura's Social Cognitive Career Theory as its theoretical framework. Figure 1 depicts research on the theory, which states that an individual creates their own world through experiences and exposure to form career aspirations in accordance with to their social and environmental surroundings (Lent, Brown, & Hackett, 2000). Social influence controls selected environments, promoting certain capabilities, ethics, and standards of living (Bandura, 2006). Such efficacy beliefs add significantly to one's level of motivation, emotional well-being, and achievements (Bandura).

One of the most important concepts of Bandura's theory is the role of human agency. Human agency relates to the individual's ability to facilitate change and self-growth. In the absence of premeditated and thoughtful conscious activity, humans are Bandura notes, simply mindless robots (Bandura, 2006). It focuses on this aspect of humans as agents who play an active or passive role in career development by controlling inner life processes (Bandura). The individual self must be socially constructed through transactional experiences with the environment (Bandura), and be a fundamental influence on their own motivation level and action in a triangle shaped system (Bandura, 1989). Accordingly, Bandura (2006) noted that human agents intentionally influence their functions and life circumstances, and directly become contributors, as opposed to byproducts of society and their environment.

According to Bandura (2006), human agency has four components: intentionality, forethought, self-reactiveness, and self-reflectiveness. Intentionality refers to purposeful actions that include plans and strategies for attaining pursuits. Forethought empowers individuals with the ability to envision goals and projected outcomes rather than be drawn by an unrealized future state; it regulates, according to Bandura (1989), the majority of human behavior and includes cognized goals, and personal goal setting by evaluation of aptitudes. Self-reactiveness implies the ability of individuals to self-regulate action plans, transforming them into moral conduct. Self-reflectiveness allows individuals to reflect on plans, self-efficacy, soundness of personal thoughts and efficacy, and re-adjustment of plans, if needed (Bandura).

Bandura understands the four aptitudes as related hierarchically (Bandura, 2006). Individuals control the social and environmental variables to ensure desired outcomes. As a result, social systems are by-products of human activity that organize, guide, and regulate human affairs (Bandura). Ultimately, if individuals are able to control aptitudes, self-governing skills, and empowering views they will be able to expand upon their career choices (Bandura). Human agency can be expressed in three modes of operation: individual, proxy, and collective (Bandura).

Individual agency notes the impacts of individuals on functioning and environment (Bandura, 2006). Proxy agency, also known as social agency, explains how individuals influence others on their behalf to achieve a desired goal for themselves (Bandura). They exercise collective agency by pooling resources and knowledge with others in order to achieve a shared goal (Bandura). The group provides mutual support, forming alliances, and working together to secure what they could not acquire on their own (Bandura, 2002). The group's shared beliefs in the collective efficacy influence the type of expectations they seek to achieve through a collective effort; usage of resources influences the effort of the collective (Bandura).

The theory calls on individuals to make sound decisions about their aptitudes, anticipated effects of events and course of action, in addition to sizing up socio-operational prospects, limitations, and regulating behavior to sustain successful outcomes (Bandura, 2006). Bandura describes the belief in personal efficacy as a central component of human agency, which empowers the individual to pursue and achieve the desired outcomes through their actions. This dissertation will address in detail the role of personal efficacy in participants' career planning processes and levels of confidence in their career goal.

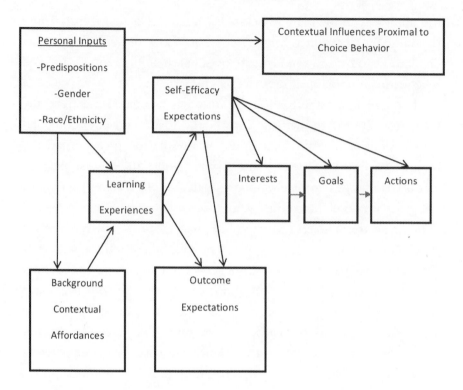

Figure 1 Diagram of Social Cognitive Career Theory

Research on Bandura's Career Theory

Patrick, Care, and Ainley (2011), in their response to Social Cognitive Career Theory, note that self-efficacy has both an independent and multiplicative effect with grades and vocational choice. The author's reading of the cross-cultural generalizability of social cognitive career theory described in Bandura's research (2002) finds that it has explanatory and predictive power to effect society-wide changes in diverse cultural milieus. Every human being has the innate foundation of human agency to survive at the level of basic capabilities, but their culture shapes their potentials into diverse forms (Bandura, 2002). The act of modeling universalizes human capacity into various different cultural milieus (Bandura). The foundation of inherent abilities, such as cultured identities, values, trust structure, and agentic abilities, make up the psychosocial systems through which familiarities are filtered (Bandura).

Two studies of Social Cognitive Career Theory (Lent, Brown, & Hackett, 2000, and Constantine, Wallace, & Kindaichi, 2005) support the application of the theory to theorizing career-related concerns for African-American students. Both state that career development is a combination of personal, contextual, and cognitive factors that influence career interest formation, goal development, and performance. The theory is predicated on three social-cognitive processes: self-efficacy beliefs, outcomes expectations, and career goals or intentions (Constantine, Wallace, & Kindaichi, 2005). Race, gender, social support, and perceived and systemic career barriers— negative contextual influences functionally related to career outcomes—affect the social-cognitive processes of career planning component for career development (Constantine, Wallace, & Kindaichi, 2005).

Constantine et al.'s (2006) study found that the incorporation of religion and spirituality in the counseling process provided insight about career choice and contributed to a purposeful and cognizant career choice for African-American adolescents. Moreover, Fouad, & Byar-Winston (2005) encouraged the inclusion of contextual factors that are influential in the career development process to identify realistic career options to produce successful outcomes.

Purpose of the Study

The purpose of this study was to explore the effects of perceived race-related stress for African-American college students at a predominately White university. Categorically, this study identified specific areas where perceived race–related stress influenced career planning for African-American college students. To date, no study has explored the positive or negative re-enforcement for African-American students who have decided to attend a predominately White university to continue their education in pursuit of a career of their choice. Chapter II's review of literature suggests a general lack of studies of the potential effects of perceived race-related stress in career planning in relation o vocational choices for African-Americans at a predominately White university.

Importance of the Study

Racism and discrimination continue to be major barriers for minorities when trying to advance in the area of academic achievement. These barriers that some African-American youth experience can lead to a sense of dispiritedness about career choices and educational attainment. Teachers' willingness to accept the negative behavior of the African-American student in the classroom setting also poses a detriment to achievement. The practice of lowered academic expectations for African-American youth on the part of instructors at both the high school and college level discourages students from developing a vocational identity that would require them to continue their education beyond high school graduation. Furthermore, the disparity of academic achievement between high school graduation and college continues to grow when compared to other ethnicities' academic achievements.

Rationale

Research has shown that negative academic experiences result in negative unwanted behavior for the African-American youth during their early school years to high school. Examples include violent behavior, aggression, substance abuse, and promiscuity. With the addition of racial discrimination in education, the African-American college student continues to suffer from race-related stress when choosing a college major or career while attending college at a predominately White university. The researcher intends to produce data that will help career counselors assist African-American college students with the process of career planning by reducing perceived race-related stress in their career development.

Research Questions

The literature regarding perceived race-related stress on African Americans and academic achievement, career planning, and vocational choice suggested the research questions that guide this study:

1. How do African-American college students at a predominately white institution perceive the race-related stress they experience?
2. What are the career expectations and perceived confidence in the achievement of their career plans of African-American college students at a predominately white institution?
3. What is the association between the participants' reported race-related stress, career planning, and career confidence?

Definition of Terms

1. *Career Barriers*—Following Swanson and Woltke (1997), this study uses the term career barriers to mean "events or conditions, either within the person or in his or her environment, that makes career progress difficult" (p.444).
2. *Career Confidence*—the individual's self-perceived resources and abilities in the completion of tasks related to the selection of a career.
3. *Career Planning*—The process through which individuals evaluate the opportunities that exist at their institution, determine their career goals, and take advantage of developmental opportunities in service to their identified goals (Sonmez, & Yildirim, 2009).
4. *Race-related stress*—Following Harrell (2000), this dissertation refers to "the race-related transactions between individuals or groups and their environment that emerge from the dynamics of racism, and that are perceived to tax or exceed existing individual and collective resources or threaten well-being" (p. 44) as race-related stress.

Summary

Chapter I provided an overview of perceived race-related stress with an emphasis on Career Planning for African-Americans. The potential effects of perceived race-related stress on the vocational achievement of this population were also presented. It also presented the theoretical framework this study will use and concluded with the purpose statement that guides research questions and definitions of relevant terms associated with the present study. Chapter II presents a discussion of the conceptual and research literature that addresses career planning and race-related stress for African-American college students.

CHAPTER II

LITERATURE REVIEW

The purpose of this study is to explore whether there is a relationship between race- related stress and the career planning process and confidence of African-American college students. Chapter II provides a review of literature related to the constructs of race-related stress, career confidence, and career planning as they relate to the experiences of African-American college students.

Career Barriers

Minority adolescents face significant educational barriers in obtaining access to certain careers. According to Constantine, Erickson, Baker, and Timberlake (1998) racial segregation may be the most significant reason that inner-city racial/ethnic minority youths have limited scholastic and occupational resources. They reveal that the U.S. high school academic system normally assigns students of color to less educationally stimulating core curriculums. They also identify a lack of a comprehensive understanding among scholars of how interventions influence students' of color's vocational development (Constantine, Erickson, Banks, & Timberlake, 1998). Other studies have found that African-American students encounter inadequate funding, a lack of introduction to various occupation selections, and inadequate contact with employed mentors in U.S. high schools (Ladany, Melincoff, Constantine, & Love, 1997; Gushue, &Whitson, 2006). Many African-American youth enter the world of work without any vocational-technical preparation, which limits their ability to compete in the job market and secure financially rewarding occupations (Constantine, Erickson, Banks, & Timberlake, 1998).

Investigations progressively validate that the effects of discrimination and race-related stress influence the distinctive experiences of minority college students (Johnson & Arbona, 2006). Numerous studies have explored career-obstacles with respect to career-associated outlooks and performances of African-American adolescents (Constantine, Wallace, & Kindaichi, 2005). For example, Ladany, Melincoff, Constantine, and Love's (1997) study discovered that perceived career obstacles are related to limited vocational investigation of career choices. They also found that at-risk urban high school students who signaled little intent to pursue college were less inclined to concern themselves about career choices and more were likely to perceive obstacles than peers in the same environment with a stronger intent to pursue college (Ladany, et. al., 1997).

A review of the literature on the issues of career development / career confidence of African-Americans college students reveals the magnitude of the race-related gap. Racism remains pervasive in the United States (Harrell, 2000) and is one of the main barriers to a lucrative career. The acceptance of how deviant behavior in the classroom can affect academic outcomes represents one manifestation of racism (O'Hara, Gibbons, Weng, Gerrard, & Simmons, 2012).

Parents try to shield their children from internalizing racism by supporting cultural and ethnic pride (Constantine Wallace, & Kindaichi, 2005). However, when students recognize that they face barriers to educational and career objectives, objective ecological factors and individuals' dynamic identification of contact with these factors collaborates to create diminished willingness to try (Lent, Brown, & Hackett, 2000). On the other hand, observing individuals achieving in spite of racial discrimination, will challenge students' notion that African-American adolescents are unwelcome in higher education or unable to achieve goals within it (O'Hara et. al., 2012). Some African-American college students still attain great career objectives and a sense of self-assurance in their capacity to manage career decision tasks in spite of the barriers they face (Constantine Wallace, & Kindaichi, 2005).

According to the most current Department of Labor Statistics report, providing data on the 1979–2002 periods, African-American high school dropouts earn $421 a week, while black college graduates earn $1,089 (U. S. Bureau of Labor Statistics, 2014). In 2009, of the 15 million African-Americans who were employed, 30 percent worked in the education and health services industries (U.S. Bureau of Labor Statistics, 2010). The Department of Labor reported that the "rate of African-Americans with a college education in the labor force increased from 16 percent in 1992 to 24 percent in 2009" (U.S. Bureau of Labor Statistics, 2010, p.5). The Bureau of Labor Statistics' (2010) report concluded that educational attainment increases potential for high earnings and lowers risk of unemployment for African-Americans generally.

According to Lent, Brown, and Hackett (2000), contemporary literature on career obstacles highlights two distinctive views: (a) students perceive obstacles, and (b) students are uncertain as to whether they believe they face obstacles. Studies in the second mold typically show no relationship between evaluations of obstacles and career results or progression factors. One study suggests African-American adolescents show greater pliability in relation to career issues generally because of their experience with racial discrimination (Constantine, Wallace, & Kindaichi, 2005). That some African-American adolescents will succeed in their career development process is certainly proven.

Career Counseling for African Americans

Career counselors must address the needs of students with many diverse ethnic viewpoints that integrate their principles, ethics, and worldviews, which makes cultural competence a significant skill (Fouad, & Winston, 2005). Fouad and Winston (2005) identify the need for specific ethnic interventions to make counseling effective (Fouad, & Winston). Researchers have developed social cognitive career theory (SCCT) as a useful approach to African-American adolescents' career decision development (Lent et. al., 2000). Contextual factors undeniably affect educational practices in conjunction with individual confidence and other types of encouragement when vocational options are formulated (Lent, Brown, & Hackett, 2000). As a result, adolescents cultivate their talents, develop personal performance criterions, and learn how to become effective when executing tasks that meet necessary expectations in regards to their performance outcomes (Lent, Brown, & Hackett, 1994).

SCCT conceptualizes career development as a union of vibrant and recurring collaborations of rational, psychosocial, and developmental issues (Lent, Brown, & Hackett, 1994). It views career growth as a blend of appropriate, individual, and intellectual factors that influence the formation of vocation awareness, goal expansion, and enactment (Lent et al., 2000). SCCT is based on three social-cognitive processes that include self-efficacy beliefs, outcome expectations, and career goals that can be shaped by race, gender, social support, in addition to perceived and systemic career barriers (Constantine, Wallace, & Kindaichi, 2005).

Similarly, Constantine, Wallace, and Kindaichi (2005) noted that systemic obstacles and inaccessibility can drive African-American adolescents' experiences of career indecision and that limited exposure to different occupations can lead them to only explore occupations that require knowledge of manual skills. Career counselors cannot understand the effects of such obstacles without recognizing how their clients experience them (Constantine, Wallace, & Kindaichi, 2005). However, Skorikov and Vondracek (1998) cautioned that using part-time employment to expose minority adolescents to different vocational choices does not necessarily affect vocational choice, although African-American adolescents might see it as an ordinary part of the introduction to the world of work.

Career counselors counseling African-American adolescents struggling with career indecisiveness should be able to identify whether indecision stems from perceived or actual obstacles, lack of information, or a combination of such factors (Ladany et. al., 1997). To do this they must be able to gauge the ways in which emotional distress influences clients' approach to education and career (Constantine & Flores, 2006).

African-American students can feel their career indecision harms their families, if younger siblings leave school because they fail to pursue or obtain a rewarding profession (Constantine & Flores, 2006).

When African-American adolescents make decisions about their careers, career counselors can then work with them to anticipate obstacles they face in obtaining their desired goals and identify support systems (Lent et. al., 2000; Constantine et. al, 1998). Fouad and Byars-Winston (2005) noted that career counselors have a duty to initiate the consideration of the sociocultural environments, such as, the effects of racism and, cultural identity, which can have emotional impact on the progression of student's career objective-setting. Constantine, Wallace, and Kindaichi (2005) suggested that career counselors should use interventions that are Afrocentric in nature for African-American adolescents in order to promote competence in educational and vocational decision-making.

Counseling practitioners must increase their knowledge about African-American college students' experiences on college campuses (Constantine et. al., 2006). They should also recognize the significant role of religion in many African-American college students' lives, to allow the expansion of psychological understandings of their career plans (Constantine et. al., 2006). Counselors should also empower African-Americans who lack a reliable support system by teaching control strategies to cope with experiences of discrimination and oppression (Constantine, Gainor, Ahluwalia, & Berkel, 2003). Such strategies might include connection with community leaders, teachers, church members, peer support, and social organizations designed to assist young African-Americans in succeeding in the world of work.

Career Planning and Implementation

Young African-Americans require support in career and college planning (O'Hara et al., 2012). Career counselors should have an understanding of the impact of home, family, and school influences, particularly in relation to at-risk students (Ladany et. al., 1997). Constantine et al.'s (2006) study concluded that recognition of religion in the counseling process contributed to a focused and conscious career choice.

The focus of implementing interventions is to promote positive encouragement of college admissions and improve academic outcomes among African-American adolescents to narrow the gap that remains in the United States (O'Hara et. al., 2012). Fouad and Byars-Winston (2005) encouraged the inclusion of contextual factors that are influential in the career development process to identify realistic career options that produce successful outcomes.

According to Constantine, Wallace, and Kindaichi's (2005) study, potentially successful intervention strategies include hosting collaborative seminars with parents and other significant people in adolescents' families and communities, focusing on teaching coping tactics in the face of racial/gender discrimination in educational and occupational settings. O'Hara et al. (2012) reported that regulated and communicative parenting facilitate family-based interventions on the part of counselors in terms of committing to future orientations. Constantine et al (2006) suggest that counselors should incorporate religious questions during initial assessment interview sessions to determine their importance in a particular client's career development. Murray et al.'s (2012) study suggests that career counselors should pair younger African-American college students with older African-American college students in a mentoring relationship that focuses on career goals.

Racism in Relation to Careers

Race-based factors impose poverty on the African-American community (Utsey & Constantine, 2008). According to Gushue and Whitson (2006), students of color may also experience obstacles such as racial/cultural discrimination that completely influence their admittance to occupational openings. Lent, Brown, and Hackett's (1994) study addressed the influence of socioeconomic circumstances on career opportunities.

In recent times, investigators have hypothesized that individuality and racial discrimination can increase or diminish racial and cultural subgroups from specific vocational goals (Fouad, & Winston, 2005). O'Hara et al.'s (2012) study noted that racial discrimination forecasts an attrition of academic opportunities that can decrease academic orientation and lead to a lower probability of college enrollment. However, Fouad and Winston's (2005) study stated that race and culture appears unconnected to career decisions, except when confounded by lack of information and/or opportunity. They also noted that young people's point of view as to the influence of race or culture on their career possibilities account for their different perceptions from white peers (Fouad & Winston, 2005). They may face economic issues or racial discrimination they did not anticipate at the outset (Lent, Brown, & Lent, 2000). The extreme effects of racial partiality and labeling may have an emotional impact on the career development of many inner-city adolescents of color (Constantine, Erickson, Baker, & Timberlake, 1998).

In spite of obstacles, African-American student may still value school and maintain high aspirations (O'Hara et al. 2012). However, their expectations for achievement may be tempered by the reality of racial obstacles (O'Hara et al. 2012). Career obstacles such as racism or race-related stress can prevent racial and cultural minorities from accomplishing their vocational objectives (Murray, Jenifer, Andrusyk, D'Angelo & King, 2012). According to Murray et al. (2012), African-American college students who adapted to Caucasian cultural principles and standards reported lower levels of occupational identity.

African-American college students who have high career aspirations and are alert to racism remain aware of their own racial and cultural identity (Murray et al., 2012). Murray et al. (2012) proposed that high career aspirations themselves lead African-American college students, correctly, to anticipate race-related obstacles in their career paths that students with lower aspirations cannot expect to face.

Perceived Race-Related Stress in Relation to Careers

Access to sources of information can affect the value of an individual's education, and certain cultures may selectively support incomplete occupationally appropriate accomplishments (Lent, Brown, & Hackett, 1994). Murray, et al. (2012) noted that stages of personality growth make the effects of race-related stress on African-American college students' career goals.

The combination of individual performance criteria and educational involvement might, furthermore, merge with communal veracities to augment or restrict educational/occupational choices (Lent, Brown, & Hackett, 1994). As the pressures from race-related stress escalate low identity growth, career goals decrease (Murray et al. 2012). Obstacles to career growth may derive from both contextually triggered forces and from internalization of these forces by the individual and resultant interpretations (Lent, Brown, & Hackett, 1994).

The same authors noted that race-related stress is a statistically substantial forecaster of African-American college students' career objectives (Murray et al. 2012). The factors of sex and culture are naturally connected to the prospective organization within which educational / career objectives are outlined and executed (Lent, Brown, & Hackett, 1994). Fouad and Winston's (2005) study noted that perceived opportunities and perceived career obstacles reflect individuals' assumptions about the organization of vocational prospects. Murray et al. (2012) noted this as well, in regards to career obstacles present in the form of racism and race-related stress, which can prevent racial and cultural subgroups from accomplishing their vocational objectives.

Theoretical Framework (SCCT/SCCT African Americans) (in relation to careers)

This section and the two that follow will discuss existent studies that used the SCCT with African-Americans. Constantine, Wallace, & Kindaichi (2005) concluded that "African- American adolescents who perceive greater career barriers tended to report higher degrees of career indecision" (p.314). Consequently, they noted that factors such as progressive racial socialization practices or even enjoying cultural self-esteem can aid as arbitrators amid perceived career obstacles and harmful career-associated drawbacks that African–Americans experience (Constantine, Wallace, & Kindaichi, 2005).

Bandura's theory states that individuals produce their personal realm through involvements and experience to create their career aspirations in accordance with their societal and environmental surroundings (Lent et al., 2000). The societal influence triggered by selected environments can continue to promote positive capabilities, ethics, and standards of living (Bandura, 2006). Lent et al. (2000) noted that a theoretical discrepancy exists, and that it concerns self-reliance in one's competency to implement a certain kind of assignment in perfect situations and confidence in one's competence to overcome impediments. Such efficacy principles add to the level of enthusiasm, expressive well-being, and performance accomplishments in a meaningful way (Bandura, 2006).

Research on Bandura's Career Theory

A review of the contemporary literature on Bandura's Social Cognitive Career Theory reveals that most studies have concentrated their focus on specific factors, without the inclusion of crucial communal, ethnic, and pecuniary issues, which can stimulate mutually cognitive-person issues and other facets of vocational performance (Lent, Brown, & Hackett, 2000). In accordance with that idea, Lent et al. (1994) note that SCCT focuses principally on background factors linked to building and executing vocational selections. In SCCT literature, Patrick, Care and Ainley (2011), noted that self-efficacy can lead to both a sovereign and a multifaceted consequence with evaluations and vocational options. Using the SCCT framework, Patrick et al. (2011) determined that the relationship between attainment and self-efficacy drives evolving occupational interests and later occupational choice.

The cross-cultural generalizability of social cognitive theory has been assessed in relation to its descriptive and prognostic power to influence civilization-wide modifications in various cultural milieus (Bandura, 2002). According to two studies, SCCT states that career development is a mixture of individual, circumstantial, and cognitive factors that influence vocational awareness development, objective progression, and performance (Lent, Brown, and Hackett, 2000, Constantine, Wallace, and Kindaichi, 2005). The theory is grounded in three social-cognitive processes—namely, self-efficacy beliefs, outcomes expectations, and career goals or intentions (Constantine, Wallace, and Kindaichi, 2005).

The processes are influenced by race, gender, and social support, in addition to perceived and systemic career barriers (Constantine, Wallace, & Kindaichi, 2005). A career barrier consists of negative circumstantial effects that an individual perceives as functionally correlated with another opportunity (Lent, Brown, & Hackett, 2000). Lindley's (2005) study reported discoveries that point out circumstantial obstacles to career expansion may be equal with proximal-process conclusion opportunities, but are reasonably distinctive from distal result opportunities.

Another important fact, according to Lindley (2005), was the frequent correspondence of the highest self-efficacy and outcome expectation score to career choice in valuable support of one of the core components of SCCT. The research studies conducted by Constantine, Wallace, and Kindaichi (2005), in addition to Lent, Brown, and Hackett (2000), reported the relevance of SCCT for theorizing career-related concerns in African-American high school students.

Main Findings

The current literature on career counseling for African-Americans has traditionally focused on the numerous challenges that affect individual, academic, and career growth (Constantine et al., 1998). O'Hara et al.'s (2005) study revealed that African-Americans who believed the United States treats African-Americans as unequal displayed inferior academic conclusion efficiency than those who believed the system was fair. In contrast, this change was absent among adolescents with robust impending orientations. Despite the despair some African-American face, O'Hara et al. (2005) reported findings that African-Americans still maintain high academic goals in the face of racial discernment.

African-Americans have disproportionately been assigned to vocational academic pathways, thus confounding their prospects to discover careers that necessitate post-secondary schooling (Constantine et.al., 1998). However, the discrepancy between career goals and career opportunities suggests that many African-Americans value education even as they believe they cannot obtain a college degree (O'Hara et al., 2005). Evidence reveals racial discrimination negatively affects college admission; moreover, a proliferation in deviancy tolerance was still substantial among those with high future orientations (O'Hara et al., 2005).

Utsey and Constantine (2008) suggested that African-Americans have developed sophisticated coping tools to deal with racism, regardless of their experiences of race-related stress. According to Constantine, Erickson, Banks, and Timberlake (1998), career counselors can have a positive impact on the career development of racial/ethnic minority youth by empowering them with significant career-development material and prospects. The insertion of variables such as racial socialization practices and institutionalized discrimination should be included in the Social Cognitive Career Theory structure to aid in the justification for the career growth of certain racial /cultural minority clusters to ponder the distinct conditions with which those members might need to deal (Lent, Brown and Hackett, 1994).

It is imperative that career counselors recognize the potential struggles present among individual and communal needs in racial/ethnic minority youth and that they implement interventions accordingly (Constantine, Erickson, Baker, & Timberlake, 1998). They should note that, as Lindley (2005) states, a college major is not an accurate signal of vocational track. Constantine and Flores (2006) noted the importance of a career counselor's ability to assess the extent of emotional anxiety concerns that could impede with vocational-associated issues to identify all-inclusive and operational mediations to correct such simultaneous problems.

Lastly, O'Hara et al. (2005) professed the idea that racial discrimination forecasts college admission through two distinctive paths, one connected with a student's academic outlook and the other connected with overall delinquent conduct. From these two pathways, African-American college students have either succeeded or failed in the realms of academia and vocational opportunities.

Summary

Chapter II presented an overview of current literature on the problems that African- American adolescents face in their career development progression from grade school to college. It also addressed the use of SCCT for assisting African-American students with career development and environmental influences and addressing career obstacles that may impair their career-decision making ability. The chapter discussed the effects of racism and perceived race-related stress on the career decision-making process, along with the use of religion as a coping mechanism that helps the African-American student counter the effects of race-related stress concerns while in pursuit of vocational attainment.

Traditional career theories have been developed for a target population of Caucasian males with western cultural views and values. Such theories were not conceptualized for use with minority clients to produce successful outcomes from career counseling sessions. Contemporary career counselors must incorporate tenets that would be beneficial to minority clients to help ensure they make proper decisions when choosing a career path.

Chapter III will present an overview of the research methodology that will structure the present study. This will include a description of the sample, research methods, ethical considerations, research instruments for data collection, and the variables, design, and statistical analysis used to test the research questions.

CHAPTER III

METHODOLOGY

Overview

The review of the literature explored the potential effects of perceived race-related stress on African Americans and their vocational and educational choices. This current chapter provides a description of the methods and procedures implemented to conduct this study. It describes the study participants and the sampling method, the variables explored, instruments of measurement and the research design. It also addresses how the research questions were measured and how data were analyzed.

Selection of Participants

The sample of the study was not probabilistic. The sample can be described as a convenience sample of African American undergraduates from a predominately White institution. Random assignment and control groups were not main characteristics of the study. Rather, convenience sampling allows the researcher to access a group of individuals who possess the characteristics that fit the requirements of this study. The participants' pool consists of African American undergraduate students enrolled at an institution in the Midwest region of North America.

These students were members of different organizations within the African- American Student Association. For the purpose of this study and to achieve the adequate statistical power of at least .70, the researcher projected the required sample size of 80 participants.

To be eligible for the study, participants had to meet the following criteria: a) currently enrolled, full- or part-time in the undergraduate program; b) aged between 18 and 24 years. The participants were contacted through the IT department of the university through its mass e-mail service.

Current events during the period of the research may have been relevant to the study's findings and may have affected recruitment. The violent deaths of unarmed black men at the hands of police in Ferguson, Mo., Baltimore, Md., Cleveland, Oh., New York, N.Y., Charleston, S.C. and at the University of Iowa were national news at the time of the recruitment and research, and artwork with racial themes was on display on campus throughout the period. .

Research Procedures

After receiving the approval from the Dissertation Prospectus Committee and the Institutional Review Board (IRB) of the University of Iowa, the researcher initially proceeded with the recruitment of the participants through the African-American Student Organizations at the institution where the research would take place. The participant recruitment process was as follows:

Stage One: Participants were contacted through the school's IT department via e-mail to African–American undergraduate students to elicit participation in the online survey on a voluntary and anonymous basis. They were notified that no compensation would be offered.

Stage Two: Each participant who expressed interest was provided the survey link via the mass e-mail to access the Qualtrics online survey. It contained the following: (a) cover letter explaining the study's purpose, consent form, and the General Information Form; (b) the Index of Race-Related Stress-Brief Version (Utsey, 1999); and (c) the Career Preparation Survey (Skorikov, 2007).

Stage Three: A correlation analysis was conducted to explore the potential association between race-related stress and the variables of career planning, career confidence, and career importance. The Statistical Package for the Social Sciences, base 22.0 (SPSS, 2014) was used to conduct the data analysis.

Research Instruments

The following section will describe the instruments used to collect the data on the effects of perceived race-related stress on career planning for African-American college students. The three instruments used in this study were: a) General Information Form, b) Career Preparation Survey (Skorikov, 2007), and c) Race-Related Stress (IRRS)—Brief Version measurement (Utsey, 1999).

General Information Form. This portion of the survey contains all the demographic information of the participants. Variables included were age, gender, academic classification, and area of study.

Career Preparation Survey. This survey was developed to observe the construction, stability, and modification of career preparation and its associations to adjustment (Skorikov, 2007). The survey comprises 20 seven-point Likert-type items measuring the predictable future of occupations and careers as well as some other questions (Porfeli & Skorikov, 2010; Skorikov, 2007). The Career Preparation Survey provides three scales that measure the status and process of career preparation in youth, which focuses on career importance, career planning, and career confidence (Porfeli & Skorikov, 2010; Skorikov, 2007).

The Career Importance Scale examines the extent to which future careers are important to young people (Porfeli & Skorikov, 2010; Skorikov, 2007). It includes of four questions that are L1, L5, L7, and L9 with scores ranging 0–24 (Skorikov, 2007). Sample items include: L1 "The occupation I have in mind is the only one I really know anything about," L5 "I don't think that my life will be strongly affected by what I will choose to do," L7 "I will only work if I have to," and L9 "I seldom think about my future occupation" (Skorikov, 2007). The Career Planning Scale assesses students' degree of involvement in the process of planning their occupational futures (Porfeli & Skorikov, 2010; Skorikov, 2007).

The Career Planning scale has eight questions, L2, L3, L6, L8, L10, L15, L18, and L19, with scores ranging 0–48 (Skorikov, 2007). Sample items include: L2 "I know what's the best career for me to pursue in the future," L3 "I feel confident that I can do well in my chosen occupation in the future," L6 "I have a plan for where I want to be in my career ten years from now," L8 "I know what to do to accomplish my occupational goals," L10 "I plan to take additional training to advance in my career," L15 "I have discussed with other people what I want for an occupation," L18 "I feel pretty good about the career I chose for myself as an adult," and L19 "I will probably have similar occupational interests twenty years from now" (Skorikov, 2007).

The Career Confidence Scale examines students' alleged ability to complete their occupational goals and achieve career success and satisfaction (Porfeli & Skorikov, 2010; Skorikov, 2007). Five questions characterize this scape, L11, L13, L14, L16, and L20, which have scores ranging 0–30 (Skorikov, 2007). Sample items include: L11 "I don't know what will be expected of me in my chosen occupation," L13 "I often question whether I have the ability to succeed in my chosen occupation," L14 "I feel that my occupational plans may be impossible to accomplish," L16 "I don't know what occupation will fit into the 'big picture' in the future," and L20 "I am not sure I will be satisfied with my future occupation."

The Career Preparation Scale is grounded in structural equations modeling, the developmental model of adolescent career preparation specified for career decidedness, planning, confidence, and importance, which ultimately fit the empirical data very well (Shorikov, 2007). The construct validity of the Career Preparation Scale was assessed using discriminant/convergent validation (Shorikov). At each time of measurement, the career planning, career confidence, and career importance scales have shown positive correlation with on another and negative correlation with career indecision (Shorikov).

As a result of the indicators of the Career Preparation survey, Shorikov (2007) stated that associations confirmed the convergent validity of the perceived scales. Overall, the patterns of associations confirm the construct validity of the Career Preparation Scale (Shorikov). The Career Planning and Career Confidence reliability coefficient was .85, which is acceptable in social sciences research.

Race-Related Stress (IRRS)—Brief Version Measurement. This instrument was developed to address the stressful experiences from routine racial encounters of African- Americans in career counseling settings (Utsey, 1999). The instrument is based on three areas of racism; namely, individual, institutional, cultural, in addition to a global racism score. Individual racism implies that one's race is superior to another race (Utsey). Institutional racism is present in policies and practices of institutions that restrict the civil rights, freedom of movement, admittance, or civil liberties of a designated race (Utsey). Cultural racism supports the idea of the individual and institutional perspective that one's race is superior over others (Utsey). The instrument has a Global Racism measure that can be computed from the scores of the three measures of the index (Lewis-Coles, & Constantine, 2006).

The instruments assess the mental and emotional welfare of African-Americans from the effects of racism and successfully discriminate between blacks and whites (Utsey). The IRRS-B is comprised of 22 items representing the Cultural racism (10 items), Institutional racism (6 items), and Individual racism (6 items), which can be administered in 5–15 minutes in clinical and research settings (Utsey). Sample items for the Cultural Racism section present statements, such as "You notice that crimes committed by White people tend to be romanticized, whereas the same crime committed by a Black person is portrayed as savagery, and the Black person who committed it, as an animal," and "You have observed the police treat White/non-Blacks with more respect and dignity than they do Blacks" (Utsey).

Sample items for the Institutional Racism section presents statements such as: "You were treated with less respect and courtesy than Whites and non-Blacks while in a store, restaurant, or other business establishments," "You have been subjected to racist jokes by White/non-Blacks in positions of authority and you did not protest for fear they might have held it against you" (Utsey). The sample items for the Individual Racism section presents statements such as: "Sales people/clerks did not say thank you or show other forms of courtesy and respect (e.g., put your things in a bag) when you shopped at some White/non-Black owned business," and "While shopping at a store the sales clerk assumed that you couldn't afford certain items (e.g., you were directed towards the items on sale)" (Utsey).

The index uses a 5-point Likert-type scale (0 = this never happened to me; 1 = this event happened, but did not bother me; 2 = this event happened and I was slightly upset; 3 = this event happened and I was upset; 4 = this event happened and I was extremely upset) (Lewis-Coles, & Constantine, 2006). The readability of the IRRS-B is estimated to be at the 9th grade reading level. The construct validity was recognized using aggregate-item confirmatory factor analysis methods that determined the best fit by a four-component oblique model (Lewis-Coles, & Constantine).

Positive and negative correlations are present among all sub-scales of the IRRS-B, together with the Global Racism measure and the RaLES-R sub-scales and global measure (Lewis-Coles, & Constantine). Accordingly, Utsey (1999) recorded adequate internal consistency reliabilities (Cronbach's alphas) for the IRRS-B: Individual Racism subscale = .78, Institutional Racism subscale = .69 and Cultural Racism subscale = .78 (Lewis-Coles, & Constantine, 2006).

Research Variables

Perceived race-related stress (cultural influences/experiences). For the purpose of this study, perceived race-related stress refers to the degree of exposure to cultural, institutional, and individual racism that can result in psychological distress (Utsey, 1999). In addition, perceived race-related stress will be operationally defined as the participant's scores to the IRRS-B, which will yield scores in four different variables (Cultural racism, Individual racism, Institutional racism, and the global racism score).

Career Planning/Career Confidence. The choice of an occupation is a solid contributing factor of an individual's status in their community, earnings, affluence, and lifestyle (Johnson, & Mortimer, 2002). As the career development process continues the individual's incentive and objectives are created that are attached to ambitions to educational achievement and occupational ambitions (Johnson, & Mortimer). Career planning, confidence, and importance will be operationally defined as a result of the participant's scores on the Career Preparation Scales.

Research Design

This study is classified as a descriptive study, which is effective in providing information on topics where there is limited research (Houser, 2009). A descriptive study is conducted to organize and describe the characteristics of a phenomenon. To collect the data, a survey design was used. In survey designs, the researcher does not manipulate an independent variable; therefore there is no concern with manipulation checks (Houser). One of the advantages of surveys is the ease of the collection of data, however, a potential disadvantage is the difficulty of getting participants to respond and return the completed questionnaire.

Research Questions

The research questions guiding the analysis were as follows.

Research Question 1: What is the perceived race-related stress of African-American college students? A descriptive analysis was conducted to describe the frequency of perceived race-related stress on career planning of African-American college students.

Research Question 2: What are the career expectations and perceived confidence in the achievement of the career plans of African-American college students? A descriptive analysis of the data will be conducted to gain information about the career planning, career confidence, and career importance of the research participants.

Research Question 3: What is the association between the participants' reported race-related stress, career planning, career confidence, and career importance and how well do individuals' career planning, career confidence, and career importance correlate with perceived race-related stress on a sample of African-American college students?

Researcher's Ethical Considerations

For this study, the researcher adhered to the guidelines of the ethical reasoning put forth by the Code of Ethics of the Commission on Rehabilitation Counselor Certification (CRCC) addressed in section I.1c: "precautions to avoid injury—rehabilitation counselors are responsible for taking precautions to avoid injuries to participants, including any psychological, emotional, physical, or social effects" (CRCC, 2009. p, 24). And in Section I.1.d: "principle researcher responsibility—the ultimate responsibility for ethical research practice lies with principal researchers. All others involved in the research activities share ethical obligations and responsibilities for their own actions" (CRCC).

In addition, the researcher assumed there was no high risk of damaging the dignity or welfare of the participants. Participants were advised by the consent form that the study would be completed on a voluntary basis and that they could withdraw at any time due to distress. Participants additionally had the option of skipping a question if they felt uncomfortable or did not wish to answer. The researcher provided his contact information in case participants wanted to contact him with concerns or issues about the study.

Summary

Chapter III presented an overview of the research methodology that structured the present study. In addition, this chapter provided a description of research participants, research procedures, the researcher's ethical considerations, and instruments for data collection, research variables, and design, and the statistical analysis used to test the research questions. Chapter IV will present the results of the data collected and the analysis of this data in addition to student organizations that were contacted for study participants.

CHAPTER IV

RESULTS

The purpose of this study was to explore the relationship of perceived race-related stress on African American college students' career importance, planning, and confidence. Therefore, the researcher sought an understanding of how perceived race-related stress may associate with the process of college students' thinking and actions as they relate to selecting a major / future career. Chapter IV presents the statistical results and theoretical implications of the findings drawn from the current preliminary investigation. It reviews the steps taken to conduct the analysis, the basic descriptive statistics, overall findings, and construct-specific results. The subsequent section reviews the data preparation steps that were necessary to conduct the statistical approach in this investigation. The specific research questions that guided this study were as follows:

1. What is the perceived race-related stress of African-American college students?
2. What are the career expectations and perceived confidence in the achievement of their career plans of African-American college students?
3. What is the association between the participants' reported race-related stress, their own career plans, and level of career confidence, and how well do individuals' career planning and

career confidence correlate with perceived race-related stress on a sample of African-American college students?

Description of Data Analyses

The outcomes of career planning, career importance, and confidence, in addition to perceived race-related stress for African-American college students, were examined using two statistical techniques: descriptive analysis and correlation analysis. Descriptive or frequency analysis is appropriate to the research questions, as it will provide a picture of the perceived race-related stress and the career planning of African-American college students. In keeping with the sample size, the researcher looked at the relationship of the variables of interest using bivariate correlation analysis to evaluate the extent of a correlation between the perceived race-related stress and career planning, importance, and confidence of the African-American college students' that are the participants of this study. The researcher used the statistical package SPSS version 22.0 to calculate the analyses.

Description of Participant Variables

The researcher received 56 on-line survey responses from a total of 562 individual members of the identified population of African-American undergraduate students from the University of Iowa. After the selection, of the 56 surveys attempted, the researcher visually explored the surveys to identify any missing data and develop a strategy to address it. A total of 43 surveys were complete and usable. This represents an approximate 7% response rate for the present study. Surveys were considered unusable when it was evident that participants completed less than 80 percent of the survey. The researcher deselected the incomplete surveys out of the Qualtrics online survey program.

The sample can be described as a convenience sample of African-American undergraduates from a predominately White institution. This sampling method does not rely on a random assignment or control groups as main characteristics of the study. Rather, convenience sampling allows the researcher to access a group of individuals who possess the characteristics that fit the requirements of this study. Descriptive statistics, the mean, standard deviation, frequency count, and frequency percentage are shown for the following demographic variables: age, gender, and classification in years, do you have a major, and major. A total of 43 African-American college undergraduate students participated. Table 1 provides information regarding participants' gender. The overrepresentation of female participants reflects some of the latest trends in college student enrollment, among African-American students. According to data from the Pew Research Center, in 2012 less than 57% of black men between the ages of 18 and 25 were enrolled in college, compared with 69% of black women in the same age group (Lopez & Gonzalez-Barrera, 2014).

Table 1: Participants' Distribution by Gender

		Frequency	Percent
Valid	Male	6	14.0
	Female	37	86.0
	Total	43	100.0

Table 2 presents the descriptive statistics for the classification in years of enrollment in college. Table 2 indicates that the majority of participants were in their 1st or 3rd year of studies.

Table 2: Participants' Distribution by Academic Classification

		Frequency	Percent
Valid	1 year	13	30.26
	2 years	8	18.6
	3 years	12	27.9
	4 years	10	23.3
	Total	43	100.0

Table 3 provides data as to participants' age.

Table 3: Participants' Distribution by Age

		Frequency	Percent
Valid	18 years old	11	25.6
	19 years old	9	20.9
	20 years old	7	16.3
	21 years old	8	18.6
	25 years old or older	8	18.6
	Total	43	100.0

Table 4 presents statistics as to whether the research participants had decided on a major area of study. Selecting a major suggests students have made some progress in career interest selection and crystallization (Super, 1994).

Table 4: Participants' Distribution by Declared Major

		Frequency	Percent
Valid	Yes	38	88.4
	No	5	11.6
	Total	43	100.0

Table 5 presents data regarding participants' selected major.

Table 5: Participants' Declared Areas of Study

	Frequency	Percent
Valid	1	2.3
Accounting	1	2.3
Applied studies in Political Science	1	2.3
Art/Jewelry & Metalsmithing	1	2.3
Biochemical engineering	1	2.3
Biology	2	4.7
Biomedical engineering	1	2.3
Biomedical Engineering	1	2.3
Bls	1	2.3
Civil Engineering	1	2.3
Communication Studies	2	4.7
Communications	1	2.3
Computer Science	1	2.3
Counselor Education	1	2.3
Elementary Education	1	2.3
Engineering	1	2.3
English	3	7.0
Global Studies Track (BLS)	1	2.3
Health and Human Physiology: Health Studies	1	2.3
Human Physiology	1	2.3
Industrial Engineering	1	2.3
Journalism	1	2.3
Mass Communication	1	2.3
Mechanical Engineering	2	4.7
Nursing	1	2.3
Open	1	2.3
OPEN	1	2.3
Political Science	2	4.7
Pre-pharmacy	1	2.3
Psychology	1	2.3
Psychology	2	4.7
Social work	1	2.3
Sociology	2	4.7
Theatre	1	2.3
Undeclared Major	1	2.3
Total	43	100.0

According to national data from the American Society for Engineering Education, for the AY 2011–2012 only 4.2% of African-American students were majoring in engineering compared to 66% White students. Data such as this prompted the researcher's question as to the role of race-related stress for African-American students.

Description of the Variables

Perceived Race-Related Stress (Cultural Influences/Experiences)

For the purpose of this study, perceived race-related stress refers to the degree of exposure to cultural, institutional, and individual racism that can result in psychological distress (Utsey, 1999). In addition, perceived race-related stress will be operationally defined as the participant's scores on the IRRS-B, which will yield scores in four different variables (cultural racism, individual racism, institutional racism, and the global racism score).

Career Importance, Planning, and Career Confidence

The choice of an occupation is a solid contributing factor of individuals' status in their community, earnings, affluence, and lifestyle (Johnson, & Mortimer, 2002). As the career development process continues, incentives and objectives are created that are attached to ambitions to educational achievement and occupational ambitions (Johnson, & Mortimer,). Career planning, confidence, and importance will be operationally defined as a result of the participant's scores on the Career Preparation Survey.

Research Question 1

Research Question 1: What is the perceived race-related stress of African-American college students? A descriptive analysis was conducted to describe the frequency of perceived race-related stress of African-American college students. The results of the analysis provided the descriptive statistics for the measures of central tendency for each of the four variables: Cultural Racism, Individual Racism, Institutional Racism, and Total Racism Score. As indicated in Table 6, the mean for the Cultural Racism Scale is 3.48 out of 10.00 with a standard deviation of .88; the Individual Racism Scale has a mean of 2.83 out of 10.00 with a standard deviation of 1.03; the Institutional Racism Scale is 2.48 out of 10.00 with a standard deviation of .90; the mean for the Race Total Score Scale was 8.80 out of 10.00 with a standard deviation of 2.52. Results suggest that the sample experienced the most race-related stress in the areas of Cultural Racism and Individual Racism. The Total Racism score indicates that collectively the sample had experienced a high degree of racism. Institutional Racism had the lowest mean.

Table 6: Participants' Perceived Race-Related Stress

	N	Mean	Std. Deviation
Cultural Racism	43	3.48	8.80
Individual Racism	43	2.83	1.03
Institutional Racism	43	2.48	.90
Race Total Score	43	8.80	2.52

Research Question 2

Research Question 2: What are the career expectations and perceived confidence in the achievement of their career plans of African-American college students? A descriptive analysis of the data was conducted to gain information about the career planning, importance and confidence of the research participants. The researcher analyzed the descriptive statistics for the average scores for all variables of interest.

Table 7: Participant's Perceived Career
Importance, Planning and Confidence

	N	Mean	Std. Deviation
Career Importance	43	5.97	.91
Career Planning	43	2.65	1.03
Career Confidence	43	5.01	1.39

Table 7 present the data related to the Career Confidence and Planning Instrument in three subscales. The mean for the Career Importance Scale was 5.97 with a standard deviation of .91; the Career Planning Scale had a mean of 2.65 with a standard deviation of 1.03; the Career Confidence Scale had a mean of 5.01 with a standard deviation of 1.39. Results from this descriptive analysis show that participants in this study had a greater understanding of the importance of the process of career selection than career planning. The fact that almost all the participants have chosen or declared a major area of study within their first three years also suggests this understanding. Although Career Confidence had inconsistency in responses, scores suggest that as a group these individuals perceived themselves as able to execute or achieve their career goals.

Research Question 3

Research Question 3: What is the association between the participants' reported race-related stress, their own career plans, and level of career confidence and how well do individuals' career planning and career confidence correlate with perceived race-related stress on a sample of African-American college students? A correlation analysis was conducted to explore a potential association between the three subscales of race-related stress, cultural racism (CR), individual racism (IR), and institutional racism (InR) and the variables of career importance (CI), career planning (CP), and career confidence (CC).

THE RELATIONSHIP BETWEEN RACE-RELATED STRESS AND THE CAREER
PLANNING AND CONFIDENCE FOR AFRICAN-AMERICAN COLLEGE STUDENTS

45

Table 8: Correlations between Index of Race-
Related Stress and Career Importance, Planning and
Confidence of African-American College Students

Variable Name		CR	IR	InR	CI	CP	CC
CR	CULTURAL_RACISM	1	.691**	.660**	.483**	-.107	-.056
IR	INDIVIDUAL_RACISM	.691**	1	.739**	.375*	-.134	.020
InR	INSTITUTIONAL_RACISM	.660**	.739**	1	.436**	-.052	-.056
CI	Career_IMP	.483**	.375*	.436**	1	-.405**	.329*
CP	Career_PLANNING	-.107	-.134	-.052	-.405**	1	-.793**
CC	Career_CONFIDENCE	-.056	.020	-.056	.329*	-.793**	1
**Correlation is significant at the 0.01 level (2-tailed).							
*Correlation is significant at the 0.05 level (2-tailed).							

The results from the analysis revealed that Cultural Racism (CR) had a strong positive relationship with Individual Racism .69 ($p<.01$) and Institutional Racism .66 ($p<.01$), and had a moderate positive relationship with Career Importance .48 ($p<.01$). Individual Racism (IR) had the strongest positive relationship with Institutional Racism .73 ($p<.01$), and had a low positive relationship with Career Importance .37 ($p<.05$). Institutional Racism (InR) had a positive moderate relationship with CI .43 ($p<.01$). Career Importance (CI) a positive low relationship with CC .39 ($p<.05$). The researcher explored the association of these variables and the participant's demographic characteristics and found no significant relationships to report.

General Findings

Participants of the present study demonstrated elements of self-efficacy (Lent, Brown, & Hackett, 2000), by the fact that the majority of them have already selected a major area of study. This suggests that the process of career selection may be well on its way from career selection to career confidence or implementation. The number of majors selected is noteworthy, as is the prevalence of majors in careers of high demand like engineering. Results from the present study also suggest that participants perceive race-related stress variables in the domains of cultural and institutional racism as having a moderate association with their career importance.

This may suggest that participants seek to consider stress experienced due to issues related to cultural and organizational racism when choosing a career. Data also suggest that race-related stress has no affect on the career confidence of African-American students who participated on this study. Anecdotal data points to the fact that many of these individuals have a strong racial identity and that various personal support groups, as well as the overall African-American community and resources available at the student's university, support this.

As a group, participants in this study do not seem prepared to or have made a plan for achieving a career path as indicated by the lower scores and negative correlations in the Career Planning area. This is an important finding and although out of the scope of this study, lack of access to resources like career counseling or guidance may be an indicator or potential explanation for this finding.

Summary

Chapter IV presented the results of the present study exploring the relationship of perceived race-related stress on African-American college students' career importance, planning, and confidence. Chapter V will present the discussion of the study findings, its limitations, and the implications for future research and rehabilitation counselor education practice.

CHAPTER V

DISCUSSION

Overview

This chapter will summarize the theoretical and practical implications of the results. It proceeds as follows: the first section discusses the findings and their relationship to previous research, the next discusses the implications and potential utilization of findings, the third section examines the study's limitations, and the fourth section provides a summary of the investigation and suggestions are offered for future research.

Restatement of the Problem

The purpose of this study was to explore the effects of perceived race-related stress associated with African-American college students who attend a predominately White institution. This study identified specific race-related stressors that influenced career planning, career confidence, and career importance for African-American college students when choosing a discipline to study. Few prior studies have explored the positive or negative factors African- American college students face specifically in relation to their career choice.

Barriers that some African American youth experience can lead to difficulty achieving career choices and educational goals. A critical factor is teachers' expectation of negative behavior of the African American student in the classroom setting. The presence of teachers who believe African American youth come to school unready and unable can have negative effects on the future career planning of their students.

Summary of Findings

The preliminary investigation provided information on race-related stress influence on career planning, career confidence, and career importance among African-American students at a large, midwestern state university. In keeping with empirical findings that exist in the literature, the study finds a relationship between race-related stress on career planning, career confidence, and career importance. The findings suggest that race-related stress affects the career planning and career confidence, as well as the sense that career is important, for African-American college students during their academic experiences and working with career counselors.

The findings also provide clarification of how perceived race-related stress can be a factor when African-American adolescents choose a career to pursue. The results of the inquiry partially support the relationship between perceived race-related stress, and career planning, career confidence, and career importance as a major contributor when choosing a career to pursue as African-American students pursue their college degree.

Participants in this study, a sample of 43 African-American students at varying levels in pursuing the college degree, responded to a demographic questionnaire, Index of Race-Related Stress- Brief Version, Career Preparatory Survey. The research questions guiding this investigation were:

1. What is the perceived race-related stress of the students in the sample?

2. What are the career expectations and perceived confidence in the achievement of the career plans of the students in the sample?

3. What is the association between the participants' reported racism-related stress, their own career plans, and career confidence and how well do individuals' career planning and career confidence correlate with perceptions of racism?

Population Sample

The investigation targeted African-American college students who are currently enrolled at a university in the Midwest of the United States of America. Five hundred sixty-two enrolled undergraduates were eligible to participate; 56 returned the survey and 43 completed it. Overall, the majority of participants (n=37) self-identified themselves as African-American female. Thirty-five were between the ages of 18 and 25.

Findings for Research Question 1

The first research question purpose was to explore the effects of perceived race-related stress for African-American college students in the areas of Cultural, Individual, and Institutional racism. The researcher used the Index of Race-Related Stress to gather this data. An analysis of descriptive statistics was conducted to assess central tendency which indicated that each sub scale had a nearly normal distribution. In summary, Cultural Racism (CR), Individual Racism (IR), and Total Racism (TR) indicate that the sample population has experienced the most race-related stress in their college setting. In other words, findings suggest that the sample population has experienced race-related stress from their own culture, personal challenges, and society as they made career-relevant decisions about their future. At the same time, results suggest that students' experiences of Institutional Racism (InR) were muted. This finding suggests that the university these students attend fosters an environment that has been effective in reducing race-related stress. The presence of Black fraternities and sororities and Black student organizations is one force that may reduce obstacles of racism and discrimination the sample population faces (Snowden, Jackson, & Flowers, 2002).

Findings for Research Question 2

The second research question explained the relationship between career expectations and perceived confidence in the achievement of the career plans of African American college students. The mean scores for Career Importance (CI) and Career Confidence (CC) are greater than Career Planning (CP) for the African-American college students that participated in the research study's on-line survey. CC refers to the individual's self-perceived resources and abilities in the completion of tasks related to the selection of a career. CP is the process through which individuals are able to evaluate the opportunities that exist at their institution, decide their career goals and take advantage of jobs, education, and other developmental opportunities to reach their identified goals (Sonmez, & Yildirim, 2009). A correlation analysis was used to determine the relationship between these two variables. The results showed a significant relationship between CI and CC. There was a negative correlation for both CI and CC in regards to CP. In other words, African-American college students in the study are persistent in their pursuit of different educational disciplines, even if they do not receive adequate career planning in the first stages of the career development process. Findings suggest they maintain their vocational focus in spite of the possibility of limited opportunity, lack of access to mentors, and, lack of resources that can help ensure degree attainment. It appears that CP and race-related stress are not good indicators as to whether an African-American college student will or will not be able to exhibit adequate educational commitment. Individuals integrate other factors in the decision to choose to pursue an educational discipline for different reasons (currency, compensation, social status in community, etc.).

As Hartung, Porfeli, and Vondracek (2005) have pointed out, CP is a multifaceted progressive process, which originates in childhood and endures through adulthood. Therefore, variability and the context in which these values are endorsed make it difficult to gain a comprehensive view of African-American college students, values, and beliefs during their career development process. Furthermore, the findings indicated that the sample population is cognizant of the importance of career selection is that many chose a career path within their first 3 years of college. Importantly, the sample population scores from the career preparation survey reflect that the participants are very confident in their ability to complete their chosen career paths. For example, their chosen majors and the timeframe used to make such decisions can reflect their confidence in their abilities about making career decisions about their futures. These findings suggest that CP may not affect CI and CC.

Findings for Research Question 3

The third research question sought to examine the association between the participants' reported Race-Related Stress, CP, CC, and CI, asking how individuals' CP, CC, and CI correlate with perceived race-related stress for the sample. The researcher conducted a correlation analysis to determine if these three variables were the best predicators of career development for African-American college student who participated in the study.

Results suggested a significant relationship between CR, IR, and InR; all three had a moderately significant relationship with CI. CR did not have a significant relationship to CP or CC. IR had a significant relationship with CR, a highly significant relationship with InR, and a non-significant relationship with CI, CP, and CC.

The results from the analysis conducted on InR found highly significant relationships with CR and IR. The relationship between InR and CI was moderately significant. InR's relationship to CP and CC was not significant. The results of the analysis on CI identified a moderately significant relationship with CR, a moderately significant relationship with IR, a moderately significant relationship with InR, and a moderately significant relationship with CC.

Analyzing CP's relationship to CR, IR, InR, CI, and CC revealed a non-significant relationship. CC displayed a slightly significant relationship with IR. CC's relationship with CI was slightly significant,

The significant relationship between CI and both IR and InR is an important finding. This is a significant finding because the sample population recognizes the barriers that they will be facing when pursuing their career choice. In conclusion, the results indicate that the sample population of African-American college students enrolled at a predominately White institution is more focused on the concepts of career importance and career confidence than the byproducts of racism and discrimination as they pursue a college degree. Results suggest that racism is important to the sample population, but evidence suggests it does not deter them in pursuing their career goals.

General Findings

Participants of the present study demonstrated elements of self-efficacy (Lent, Brown, & Hackett, 2000), because the majority of the participants had selected a major area of study. This suggests that the process of career selection was well on its way from career selection to career confidence or implementation prior to this study. It is noteworthy that many of the majors that the survey participants selected will prepare them for occupations that are in high demand, like engineering. Results also suggest that participants perceive CR and IR as moderately significant for CI. This suggests that participants consider anticipated experiences of racism as an important factor in their career choice. Data also suggest that race-related stress has no bearing affect on CC among students in the sample. Anecdotal evidence suggests that many of participants may have a strong racial identity and that personal support groups as well as the overall African-American community and resources available at their school support this identity, including black student organizations, black Greek organizations, and mentoring.

As a group, participants in this study have low scores in CP. Results suggest that participants have chosen occupations with a high employment outlook but have failed to engage in extra-curricular activities that lead to entry-level employment post-graduation, and that race-related stress may be part of this failure.

Interpreting the Data through the Theory

Bandura's Social Cognitive Career Theory (SCCT) states that individuals create their own world through experiences and exposure and that they form their career aspirations in accordance to their social and environmental surroundings (Lent, Brown, & Hackett, 2000). Results of this study suggest that participants recognize the relationship between cultural factors and career importance. In other words, they understand the contributions cultural and organizational-racial factors may have to their career outlook. The sample participants displayed high self-efficacy, demonstrated by their career confidence scores, which may increase one's level of motivation, emotional welfare, and achievement of goals (Lent, Brown, & Hackett, 2000).

According to Lent, Brown, and Hackett (2000) SCCT places emphasis on cognitive-person variables that are identified as self-efficacy, outcome expectations, and goals that intermingle with the individual's environment such as gender, culture, social supports, and obstacles. Furthermore, the sample population has modeled the three components of SCCT that have been beneficial to their development through the progression of their career development process. As a result, the sample population has been able to exercise their personal control which is also known as human agency (Lent, Brown, & Hackett). For example, other factors for consideration for the sample population include their physical attributes, such as sex, race, features of the environment, and learning experiences (Lent, Brown, & Hackett, 2000). In brief, these factors influence career-related interests and choice behavior of individuals (Lent, Brown, & Hackett). In accordance, with the theory, the sample population's response to their environment is solely based on their educational experiences and the accessibility of financial resources to pursue training options which will affect their career development (Lent, Brown, & Hackett, 2000).

Lent et al. (2000) point out that the background contextual factors that affect the learning experiences of individuals and therefore mold their career-relevant self-efficacy and outcome expectations include career role models. Further, proximal environmental factors can discreetly and unswervingly affect the developments that help individuals decide and implement career-relevant choices (Lent, Brown, & Hackett, 2000). In fact, these procedures can influence the relationships of interests to pick goals, and goals to actions (Lent, Brown, & Hackett). Additionally, the level of support and discouragement individuals experience in pursuing particular academic and extracurricular activities help influence individuals' career development process (Lent, Brown, & Hackett, 2000).

Results suggest that participants experience IR and InR as related, and that both affect CI. Ultimately, however, CI and CC engaged the participants more than any form of racism in their pursuit of a college degree. While racism is important to the sample population it was not significant enough to deter them in viewing careers and important and feeling confident about it, although it may be derailing their planning activities.

Summary

Darcy and Brown (2008) noted the continued significance of race in civic and social contexts and the fact that higher education researchers and policy makers have yet to address these issues and concerns to develop guidelines that will produce more successful outcomes for the assessment, interpretation, and intervention of race in colleges, schools, or social institutions. To begin with, Snowden, Jackson, and Flowers (2002) have noted that the educational attainments of African-American students are lesser than their White peers on campus mainly due to adjustment difficulties. In particular, the same authors posited that African-American students have shown an amplified rate of attrition, less significant grade point averages, and less significant post-graduate matriculations than White peers. Many colleges and universities offer African-American fraternities and sororities (Snowden, Jackson, and Flowers, 2002), Black student organizations and other structures that have been beneficial to students (Osegura, 2005) to battle emotions of isolation, alienation, and lack of support (Snowden, Jackson, and Flowers, 2002).

In other words, African-Americans do face many numerous contextual factors in college. Moreover, there is a clear distinction between the differences between students attending historically Black colleges and universities and those who attend predominately White institutions. For instance, authors Caldwell and Obasi (2010) concede that past research suggests that the racial composition of college or university has a significant effect on learning outcomes; they proposed that attendance at a historically Black college or university (HBCU) significantly enriches the academic and social growth of African-American students above predominant White institutions (PWIs). Measures of gains in personal and social development, the arts and humanities, science and technology, and gains in intellectual and writing skills support these findings (Caldwell & Obasi, 2010).

Caldwell and Obasi's (2010) study shows that the success of the integration of constructs specific to African-American students into the SCCT model. Their study observed cultural mistrust (a perceived barrier), educational value (an outcome expectation), and achievement motivation (an extension of self-efficacy) in relation to academic performance on a college level in a sample of 202 African-American students. They found that achievement motivation, cultural mistrust, and educational value differed for students attending HBCUs versus PWIs.

Gossett, Cuyjet, and Cockriel (1998) recognized that African-Americans at PWIs frequently felt burdened in the classroom by the obligation to speak on behalf of their entire race, and posited that this might have an impact on their achievement. Such experiences fuel passionate stress categorized by being passive about speaking up in class; impersonal institutions typically cannot create environments that are conducive to student involvement and growth as smaller personal institutions (Oseguera, 2005). These findings suggest career counselors must combat the large gap of education attainment and occupational opportunities among African- Americans and other ethnicities.

The education community in general and career counselors specifically have an opportunity to be a part of the solution to the problems African-American students face in planning to join the middle or upper middle class after college. This study has focused on career counselors' obligation to help warrant that African-American clients that do seek career counseling services are empowered with the best opportunity to succeed. In brief, career counselors can assist through concentrated hard work that has been beneficial to African-Americans with vigorous career development to promote equality of earnings and long term employment.

For the participants in this study, racism is interwoven through their daily life activities and academia. They will face race-related stress in the world of work. Race-related stress affects the individual, institutional, and cultural. Individual stress exists in the form of social economic status (SES), level of parental education, role model/mentoring, and occupational exposure. Institutional stress appears in the form of low support or encouragement to chase vocational careers that require higher education training due to discrimination because of ethnic/race identity. Cultural stress appears in the form of an individual's cultural perspective on education and certain professions.

Existing research on career planning and career counseling (Harro, 2010) have comprehensively documented the impact of environments, such as schools, on the perpetuation of behavioral attitudes like discrimination and racism. Early racial discrimination experiences in school settings can lead African Americans to believe that education will not provide them any benefit because of the racial barriers they will face in employment upon graduation (O'Hara et. al., 2011). Consequently, the effects of such experiences have led many African-American students to academic underachievement and low participation in higher education.

Therefore, it has become of great importance to rehabilitation, school, and college counselors who understand the effects of racism on the lives of African-Americans. The effects of stress-related experiences of racism on career goals are an area of particular importance. The researcher conducted a preliminary investigation on the perceived race-related stressors that African-American college students confront in a PWI and the effects on career aspirations and level of confidence in their career plans. Overall, the results of this preliminary investigation provide evidence that CI and CC are very important in the career development process of African-American college students. It appears that career counselors are more likely to include variables or values in counseling sessions with African-American students if they perceive a match between their own values and the students'.

Limitations of the Study

There were limitations to this preliminary investigation. The most notable limitations are (a) small number of participants, (b) survey sampling and distribution method, and (c) variance within sample. Specifically, a convenience sample consisting of 43 students does not provide results that can be generalized to the population of all African-American undergraduate college students. Further, the sample was drawn from only one school in the United States.

The sample was disproportionately female (over 84.2%), which potentially also limits the generalizability of the results. While research suggests the population of African American college students is also disproportionately female (Lopez & Gonzalez-Barrera, 2014), there was not enough power in the sample to adequately test for outcome variances in fit between race-related stress and career development concepts. A larger sample size that reflected scores from participants from a number of PWIs would likely provide more generalizable results.

A second limitation was that the survey was disseminated via a mass email system which provided the link to the school's Qualtrics ™ system. The use of a convenience sampling of the population, and distribution of the survey to all eligible African-American college students at a single university, did not permit comparison of respondents and non-respondents. The researcher faced several challenges in collecting data that contributed to this limitation; participation rates were low.

Implications for Future Research

First, implication for future research includes the fact that the findings of resilience by some African-Americans in regards to race-related stress in career development activities might prompt investigations into the mechanisms of that resilience. Researchers might consider both environmental and personal factors. Research might guide career counselors in deciding whether, to empower better choices when making career decisions, to focus in sessions more on students' environment or personal issues and concerns. Future research might also address how institutions can attract students who perceive that they will have IR and therefore select another college.

A third area for future research is the practical applications of Bandura's Theory for Master's level counselors when working with African-American college students? The study was investigative; therefore, replication of this investigation with a larger and a more heterogeneous sample would be a clear avenue for future research, as would additional explorations of the role that race-related influence in the career development process for African-American adolescents and young adults.

Future research might also investigate the findings' relationship to prior research. Johnson and Arbona (2006) indicated that research gradually authenticated the effects of discrimination and race-related stress impact the distinguishing experiences of minority college students. Ladany, Melincoff, Constantine, and Love's (1997) study noted that vulnerable inner-city high school students did not possess the intent to pursue college, were less concerned about career choices, and were more likely to perceive obstacles. The current study differs from these studies in that the sample population clearly is focused on choosing the right career path, and possesses a high level of confidence that they will attain their goals.

In general, there is ample room for new research into career counseling for diverse student bodies. Career theories that guide career counselors were developed for a target population of Caucasian males, with western cultural views and values. These theories were not conceptualized for use with minority students to produce successful outcomes from career counseling sessions. The current career counselor has to incorporate tenets that would be beneficial to minority clients to help ensure they make proper decisions when choosing a career path, and studies such as this one have the potential to aid in that process.

Future studies should consider investigating whether the lack of career planning would be detrimental to the entire career development process for African-American adolescents and young adults from communities, and educational districts with scare resources, and bad educational experiences. It is possible that conventional career development is not a key part of creating a successful career after college. Participants in the current study value CI and CC. Future research might assess the importance and impact of this.

Conclusion

This investigation examined the relationship between race-related stress effects on career development for the African-American college students. The findings may help career counselors to better serve minority populations. Chapter V presented a discussion of the results associated with the examination of the relationship between race-related stress and the components of the career development process that can be of some benefit to career counselors, whether they are positive or negative. The results indicated that career importance is a meaningful concept as it relates to facilitating positive outcomes for career development for African-American college students. Besides, lack of uniformity universally in the sample group presents problems for the career counselors, which make it difficult to develop a plan for any individual from such population. Constantine, Erickson, Banks, and Timberlake (1998) inferred from the harsh veracity of the African-American adolescents in their sample that the numerous impediments they face disrupt their occupational decision-making progress and career development. The current study shows that African-American college students in a PWI can possess the resiliency and determination needed to pursue careers even in the face of race-related stress obstacles. The inclusion of cultural identity, social support, and available resources has enabled to African-American college student to withstand the effects of racism in college. Still, better career development experiences can only benefit this population and thereby address social disparities.

REFERENCES

Alfred, M. (2001). Expanding theories of career development: adding the voices of African American women in the white academy. Adult Education Quarterly, 51.108-127. DOI: 10.1177/07417130122087179

Bandura, A. (1989). Human agency in social cognitive theory. *American Psychologist, 44,* 1175-1184.

Bandura, A. (2002). Social cognitive theory in cultural context. *Applied Psychology: an International review.51,* 269-290.

Bandura, A. (2006). Toward a psychology of human agency. *Perspectives on Psychological Science, 1,*164-180. DOI: 10.1111/j.1745-6916.2006.00011.x.

Bingham, R.P., Ward, C.M., Butler, M.M. (2006). Career counseling with African American women. Handbook of Career Counseling for Women (2nd ed.)Bruce, W. (Ed); Heppner, M.J. (Ed) (2006). Contemporary topics in vocational psychology, (pp. 219-239).

Mahwah, NJ, US: Lawrence Erlbaum Associates publishers, x, 553pp.

Commission on Rehabilitation Counselor Certification. (2009). Code of professional ethics for rehabilitation counselors. Schaumburg, IL: Author.

Constantine, M.G., Erickson, C.D., Banks, R.W., & Timberlake, T.L., (1998). Challenges to the

Career development of urban racial and ethnic minority youths: Implications for vocational intervention. Journal of Multicultural Counseling and Development, 26, 83- 95.

Constantine, M.G., Gainor, K.A., Ahulwalia, M.K., & Berkel, L.A., (2003). Independent and Interdependent self-construal, individualism, collectivism, and harmony control in African Americans. The Journal of Black Psychology, 229, 87-101.

Constantine, M.G., Lewis, E. L., Conner, L.C., & Sanchez, D., (2000). Addressing spiritual and religious issues in counseling African American: Implications for counselor training and practice. Counseling and Values, 45, 28-39.

Constatine, M. G., Milville, M.L., Warren, A.K., Gainor, K.A., and Lewis-Coles, M. E.L. (2006) religion, spirituality, and career development in African american college students: a qualitative inquiry. *The Career Development Quarterly, 54,* 227-241.

Constatine, M.G., Wallace, B.C., and Kindaichi, M.M. (2005) Examining contextual factors in the career decision status of african american adolescents, *Journal of Career Assessment, 13,* 307-317. DOI: 10.1177/1069072705274960.

Fouad, N. A., & Byars-Winston, A.M. (2005). Cultural context of career choice: meta-analysis of race/ ethnicity differences. *The Career Development Quarterly, 53,* 223-233.

Gomstyn, A. (2003). Minority enrollment in colleges more than doubled in past 20 years, study finds. The Chronicle of Higher Education.com. Retrieved 08/23/2013 from http://chronicle.com/article/Minority-Enrollment-in/111294/

Harrell, S. P. (2000). A multidimensional conceptualization of racism-related stress: Implications for the well-being of people of color. *American Journal of Orthopsychiatry, 70,* 42-57.

Harro, B. (2010) the cycle of socialization. In Adams, M., Blumenfeld, W.J., Castaneda, C.A.,

Hackman, H. W., Peters, M.L., and Zuniga, X.(Eds.) *Readings for diversity and social justice 2nd ed.* (pp. 45-52). New York: Rutledge

Hendricks, F. M. (1994) Career counseling with African American college students. *The Journal of Career Development, 21,*117-126.

Johnson, M. K., & Mortimer, J. T., (2002). Career choice and development from a sociological perspective. In Career Choice and Development /Duane Brown and associates-4th Ed.p.cm.- (The Jossey –Bass business & management series).3rd ed. c1996. rev.ed.of:

Career choice and development/ Duane Brown, Linda Brooks, and associates. 37-84.

Ladany, N., Melincoff, D.S., Constantine, M.G., & Love, R., (1997). At- risk urban high school Students' commitment to career choices. Journal of Counseling and Development, 76, 45-52.

Lent, R.W. (2013) Career- life preparedness: revisiting career planning and adjustment in the new workplace. *The Career Development Quarterly, 61,* 2-14. DOI:10.1002/j.2161-0045.2013.00031.x

Lent, R.W., Brown, S.D., & Hackett, G., (1994). Toward a unified social cognitive theory of career and academic interest, choice, and performance. Journal of Vocational Behavior, 45, 79-122.

Lent, R. W., Brown, S. D., & Hackett, G. (2000) Contextual supports and barriers to career choice: a social cognitive analysis. *The Journal of Counseling Psychology, 47,* 36-49.

Lewis-Coles, M.E., & Constantine, M.G. (2006). Racism-related stress, africultural coping, and religious problem-solving among African Americans. Cultural Diversity and Ethnicity

Lopez, M.H., and Gonzalez-Barrera, A., (2014). Women's college enrollment gains leave men behind. Retrieved 04/13/2015 from: http://www.pweresearch.org/fact-tank/2014/03/06/womens-college-enrollment

Lutz, J.G., & Eckert, T.I., (1994). The relationship between canonical correlational analysis and multivariate multiple regression. Educational and psychological Measurement, 54,666-675. Minority Psychology, 12, 433-443.

Lyn, P., Care, E., and Ainley, M. (2011) the relationship between vocational interests, self-efficacy, and achievement in the prediction of educational pathways. *The Journal of Career Assesment, 19,* 61-74.

Matthews-Armstead, E. (2002). And they still rise: college enrollment of African American women from poor communities. Journal of Black Studies, 33, 44-65. DOI: 10.1177/002193470203300103.

Murray, D. T., Jenifer, E.S., Andrusyk, J.J., D'Angelo, R., & King, T., (2012). Racism-related stress and ethnic identity as determinants of African American college students' career aspirations. The Career Development Quarterly, 60,254-262.

O'Hara, R. E., Gibbons, F.X., Weng, C.Y., Gerrard, M., and Simmons, R.L. (2011). Perceived racial discrimination as a barrier to college enrollment for African Americans. *Personality and Social Psychology Bulletin, 38,* 77-90. DOI: 10.1177/0146167211420732.

Parham, T. A., and Austin, A.L. (1994). Career Development and African Americans: a contextual reappraisal using the nigrescence construct. *Journal of Vocational Behavior, 44,139*-154.

Pope, M. (2009) Jessie Buttrick Davis (1871-1955); Pioneer of vocational guidance in the Schools. *Career Development Quarterly, 57,*278-288.

Porfeli, E. & Skorikov, V. (2010). Specific and diversive career exploration during late Adolescence. Journal of Career Assessment, 18, 46-58.Schmidt, P. (2008). Colleges seek key to success of black men in classroom. The Chronicle of Higher Education.com. Retrieved 08/23/2013 from http:// chronicle.com/article/ Colleges-Seek-Key-to – Success/27296/.

Shaw, K. M., & Coleman, A.B., (2000). Humble on Sundays: family, friends, and faculty in the Upward mobility experiences of African American females. Anthropology and Education Quarterly 31,449-470.

Shorter-Gooden, K. (2004). Multiple resistance strategies: how African American women cope with racism and sexism. Journal of Black Psychology, 30, 406-425.

Skorikov, V. (2007). Continuity in adolescent career preparation and its effects on adjustment. Journal of Vocational Behavior,70,8-24. doi:10.106/jvb.2006.04.007.

SPSS. (2005). Statistical package for the social sciences base 12.0 application guide. Chicago: Author.

Sonmez, B. and Yildirim, A., (2009) what are the career planning and development practices for nurses in hospitals? Is there a difference between private and public hospitals? *Journal of Clinical Nursing, 18, 3461-3471.*

Sue, D. W., (1977) Counseling the culturally different: a conceptual analysis. *Personal & Guidance Journal, 55,422-446.*

Super, D. E. (1994). A life-span, life-space perspective on convergence. In M. L. Savickas & R. W. Lent (Eds.), *Convergence in career development theories.* Alto, CA: Consulting Psychologists Press.

Swanson, J. L., & Woitke, M. B. (1997). Theory into practice in career assessment for women: Assessment and interventions regarding perceived barriers. *Journal of Career Assessment, 5,* 443-462.

Sykes, A.O., (1986). An introduction to regression analysis. Retrieved June 7, 2013 from: www.law.uchicago.edu/files/files/20. Sykes_.Regression.pdf.

Tovar-Murray, D., Jenifer E. S., Andrusyk, J., D'Angelo, R., & King, T. (2012). Racism-related stress and ethnic identity as determinants of African American college students' career aspirations. *The Career Development Quarterly, 60,* 254-262.

U.S. Department of Labor, Bureau of Labor Statistics (2007). Women in the labor force: A Databook (Report 1002). Retrieved from http: //www.bls.gov/cps/wlf-databook2007.htm.

Utsey, S. O., and Ponterotto, J.G. (1996) Development and validation of the race-related stress (IRRS). *Journal of Counseling Psychology, 43,* 490-501.

Utsey, S. (1999). Development and validation of a short form of the index of race-related stress (IRRS)-brief version. Measurement &Evaluation in Counseling and Development, 32, p.149-172.

Walton, G. M., and Cohen, G. L. (2011) a brief social-belonging intervention improves academic and health outcomes of minority students. *Science, 331, 1447*-1451.

Hartung, P. J., Porfeli, E. J., & Vondracek, F. W., (2005). Child vocational development: A review and reconsideration. *Journal of Vocational behavior. 66,* 385-419. doi:10.1016/j.jvb.2004.05.006

Snowden, M.T., Jackson, J.F.L., & Flowers, L.A., (2000). An examination of the efficiency of the proposed remedies and settlement for Ayers: Based on a study of black college students in Mississippi. *NASAPJournal, 7, 7*-20.

APPENDIX A

INDEX OF RACE-RELATED
STRESS—BRIEF VERSION

Instructions

This survey questionnaire is intended to sample some of the experiences that Black people have in this country because of their "blackness." There are many experiences that a Black person can have in this country because of his/her race. Some events happen just once, some more often, while others may happen frequently. Below you will find listed some of these experiences, for which you are to indicate those that have happened to you or someone very close to you (i.e., a family member or loved one). It is important to note that a person can be affected by those events that happen to people close to them; this is why you are asked to consider such events as applying to your experiences when you complete this questionnaire. Please circle the number on the scale (0 to 4) that indicates the reaction you had to the event at the time it happened. Do not leave any items blank. If an event has happened more than once, refer to the first time it happened. If an event did not happen, circle 0 and go on to the next item.

0 = this never happened to me.
1 = this event happened, but did not bother me.
2 = this event happened & I was slightly upset.
3 = this event happened & I was upset.
4 = this event happened & I was extremely upset.

1. You notice that crimes committed by White people tend to be romanticized, whereas the same crime committed by a Black person is portrayed as savagery, and the Black person who committed it, as an animal.

   0   1   2   3   4

2. Sales people/clerks did not say thank you or show other forms of courtesy and respect (e.g., put your things in a bag) when you shopped at some White/ non-Black owned businesses.

   0   1   2   3   4

3. You notice that when Black people are killed by the police, the media informs the public of the victim's criminal record or negative information in their background, suggesting they got what they deserved.

   0   1   2   3   4

4. You have been threatened with physical violence by an individual or group o f White / non- Blacks.

   0   1   2   3   4

5. You have observed that White kids who commit violent crimes are portrayed as "boys being boys," while Black kids who commit similar crimes are wild animals.

   0   1   2   3   4

6. You seldom hear or read anything positive about Black people on radio, TV, in newspapers, or history books.

   0   1   2   3   4

7. While shopping at a store the sales clerk assumed that you couldn't afford certain items (e.g., you were directed toward the items on sale).

   0   1   2   3   4

8. You were the victim of a crime and the police treated you as if you should just accept it as part of being Black.

   0   1   2   3   4

9. You were treated with less respect and courtesy than Whites and other non-Blacks while in a store, restaurant, or other business establishment.

   0   1   2   3   4

10. You were passed over for an important project although you were more qualified and competent than the White/non-Black person given the task.

    0   1   2   3   4

11. Whites/non Blacks have stared at you as if you didn't belong in the same place with them; whether it was a restaurant, theater, or other place of business.

    0   1   2   3   4

12. You have observed the police treat White/non-Blacks with more respect and dignity than they do Blacks.

0   1   2   3   4

13. You have been subjected to racist jokes by Whites/non-Blacks in positions of authority and you did not protest for fear they might have held it against you.

0   1   2   3   4

14. While shopping at a store, or when attempting to make a purchase, you were ignored as if you were not a serious customer or didn't have any money.

0   1   2   3   4

15. You have observed situations where other Blacks were treated harshly or unfairly by Whites/non-Blacks due to their race.

0   1   2   3   4

16. You have heard reports of White people/non-Blacks who have committed crimes and in an effort to cover up their deeds falsely reported that a Black man was responsible for the crime.

0   1   2   3   4

17. You notice that the media plays up those stories that cast Blacks in negative ways (child abusers, rapists, muggers, etc.), usually accompanied by a large picture of a Black person looking angry or disturbed.

0   1   2   3   4

18. You have heard racist remarks or comments about Black people spoken with Impunity by White public officials or other influential White people.

0   1   2   3   4

19. You have been given more work, or the most undesirable jobs at your place of employment while the White/non-Black of equal or less seniority and credentials is given less work, and more desirable tasks.

0   1   2   3   4

20. You have heard or seen other Black people express a desire to be White or to have White physical characteristics because they disliked being Black or thought it was ugly.

0   1   2   3   4

21. White people or other non-Blacks have treated you as if you were unintelligent and needed things explained to you slowly or numerous times.

0   1   2   3   4

22. You were refused an apartment or other housing; you suspect it was because you're Black.

0   1   2   3   4

Source: Utsey, S.O. (1999) Development and Validation of a short form of the Index of Race-Related Stress (IRRS)—Brief Version, Measurement and Evaluation in Counseling and Development, (3), 149-167.

Career Preparatory Survey

SECTION L. Some young people make up their minds about their future. There are many important things one might think about, but the one that we all have to decide upon is our occupational future. Even those who choose to become a homemaker make an occupational choice. In this section we ask you to think about an occupation or career you picture for yourself in the future (after you complete all the necessary education and training), 10 or even 20 years from now. For each statement below, mark one answer between the 'disagree' and 'agree'. A "3" means either completely agree or completely disagree, whereas a "0" means unsure; ones and twos indicate moderate degrees of either agreement or disagreement.

		Agree					Disagree	

L1. The occupation I have in mind is the only one I really know anything about.　　0　1　2　3　4　5　6

L2. I know what's the best career for me to pursue in the future.　　0　1　2　3　4　5　6

L3. I feel confident that I can do well in my chosen occupation in the future.　　0　1　2　3　4　5　6

L4. I don't know if there's the right career for me.　　0　1　2　3　4　5　6

L5. I don't think that my life will be strongly affected by what I will choose to do.　　0　1　2　3　4　5　6

L6. I have a plan for where I want to be in my career ten years from now.　　0　1　2　3　4　5　6

L7. I will only work if I have to.　　0　1　2　3　4　5　6

L8. I know what to do to accomplish my occupational goals.　　0　1　2　3　4　5　6

L9. I seldom think about my future occupation.   0 1 2 3 4 5 6

L10. I plan to take additional training to advance in   0 1 2 3 4 5 6
my career.

L11. I don't know what will be expected of me in my   0 1 2 3 4 5 6
chosen occupation.

L12. My future occupation is important to me as a way   0 1 2 3 4 5 6
of life.

L13. I often question whether I have the ability to   0 1 2 3 4 5 6
succeed in my chosen occupation.

L14. I feel that my occupational plans may be impossible   0 1 2 3 4 5 6
to accomplish

L15. I have discussed with other people what I want for   0 1 2 3 4 5 6
an occupation.

L16. I don't know what occupation will fit into the 'big   0 1 2 3 4 5 6
picture' in the future.

L17. I will use what I learn in school to advance in my   0 1 2 3 4 5 6
future career.

L18. I feel pretty good about the career I choose for   0 1 2 3 4 5 6
myself as an adult.

L19. I will probably have similar occupational interests   0 1 2 3 4 5 6
twenty years from now.

L20. I am not sure I will be satisfied with my future   0 1 2 3 4 5 6
occupation.

Source: Skorikov, V. (2007). Continuity in adolescent career preparation and its effects on adjustment. Journal of Vocational Behavior,70, 8-24. doi: 10.106/ jvb.2006.04.007

APPENDIX B

(Diagram of Social Cognitive Career Theory)

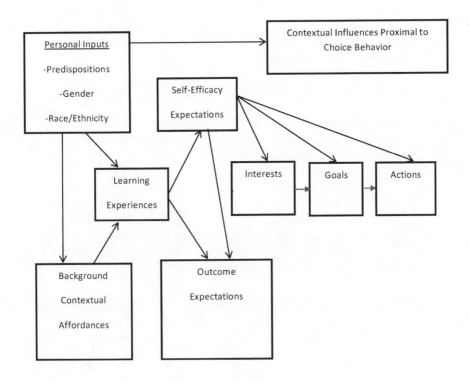

Social Cognitive Career Theory
(Lent, Brown & Hackett, 1994, 2000)

Printed in the United States
By Bookmasters